To Tom.

Much Lo...

Mum

Christmas 1989

£4

BUSES
YEAR BOOK 1990

BUSES
YEAR BOOK 1990
Edited by Stewart J. Brown

LONDON

IAN ALLAN LTD

First published 1989

ISBN 0 7110 1866 9

Published by Ian Allan Ltd,
Shepperton, Surrey; and printed by
Ian Allan Printing Ltd at their
works at Coombelands in
Runnymede, England

Front cover:
**Lothian Region Transport's
Leyland Atlantean PDR1A/1
photographed in Hanover
Street, Edinburgh on 27 March
1988. This vehicle, fleet No 267,
was withdrawn from service the
following month.** *John Allison*

Back cover:
**RT2799 is operated by Blue
Triangle and is seen here at
Hatfield Heath on 10 April
1988.** *R. J. Waterhouse*

Contents

Stewart J. Brown

Single-Deck Revival?

The 1990s start with renewed interest in 11-metre long single-deck city buses. **Stewart J. Brown** *looks at the trend and asks if double-deckers are on the way out.*

Will the 1990s see a single-deck bus revival? Is the double-deck bus, that peculiarly British beast, facing extinction? What can be read into sales of the Leyland Lynx doubling annually?

Britain's bus builders are entering the 1990s with a rash of new citybus models — and all are single-deckers. Leyland's Lynx is a product of the mid-1980s and is young enough to be seen as a new model, the first of a new generation of *fin de siècle* city buses. DAF's new SB220 made its appearance in the UK market in 1988, along with Renault's ageing PR100. Scania is selling the new K93 and N113, also launched in 1988, and Iveco plans to sell its city bus chassis in Britain in the 1990s.

The approach of 1992 and the single European market could signal the opportunity for bus builders to sell their wares in as many markets as they can. And the most widely-accepted form of citybus in Europe is the single-decker.

Britain has of course seen bursts of interest in single-deck citybuses before. But from the early 1930s to the early 1960s single-deck buses were a rare sight on urban services. Before the single deck boom of the 1960s operators running high-frequency urban services did so with double-deckers wherever possible.

The first inkling of interest in high-capacity single-deckers came when 11-metre (m) long single-deckers were legalised in 1961 and one of the first was a Leyland Leopard bus for Edinburgh City Transport with a three-door Alexander body. Passengers entered at the rear, paid a seated conductor, and left by either the centre or front exit. Seated conductors were a short-lived novelty, and Edinburgh's three-door Leopard remained unique.

The real attraction for city operators was the rear-engined single-decker which offered relatively easy access (although step heights were not then the major issue which they became in the 1970s) and a low floor. But on top of all this it allowed one-man operation, offering considerable scope for cost savings.

Or so it seemed until operators discovered just how expensive rear-engined single-deckers really were. Expensive to buy, expensive to fuel, expensive to repair and expensive to dispose of since many were short-lived and not fully depreciated.

A number of urban operators burned their fingers in the 1960s. Sunderland Corporation opted not only for single-deckers but also for a continental-style flat fare. London Transport announced a grand reshaping plan and bought its ill-starred AEC Merlins and Swifts which were quickly discarded. Liverpool, Leeds, Manchester, Aberdeen, Preston, Blackpool, Lincoln and Great Yarmouth all tried single-deckers in the 1960s — soon reverted to double-deckers.

The integral Leyland National was a product of the city operators' optimism that the single-decker was the bus of the future — but by the time it appeared in 1972 the optimism had vanished and production peaked at 20 a week, only half of that originally planned.

So what's different in the 1990s?

For a start, buses are generally less busy. Local bus use has dropped dramatically in the past 20 years — and 1986's deregulation has not stopped the decline — so many operators are now considering whether or not they really need to run double-deck buses.

Then there is the competitive environment created by deregulation. Some operators see single-deckers as giving them a marketing advantage over those who run traditional double-deckers. Most current double-deck body designs may be very attractive but none have the panache of the new generation of single-deckers.

5

Or there is the convenience: no stairs to climb, making virtually all of the seats accessible to passengers who may be encumbered with shopping, or who may be old and relatively lacking in agility. The negative side of this is that there are of course fewer seats in total so more peak period travellers have to stand.

A telling argument relates to vandalism. The top deck of a double-decker attracts a lot of unwanted attention from the undesirables in our midst which makes it an unattractive area for passengers and involves operators in expensive repair work. Vandalism is much reduced in single-deckers because every passenger is within the driver's view.

But there is also an element of necessity being the mother of invention: DAF and Renault do not build double-deck chassis. If they want to sell in Britain, they have to promote single-deckers. And Scania's K and N-series underframes were conceived as single-deckers although both have been fitted with double-deck bodywork.

Leyland's Lynx is the longest-established of the new generation single-deckers, having been launched in 1985. The first complete British Lynx entered service with West Midlands PTE in 1986 and was quickly followed by examples for AA of Ayr, Colchester, Fishwick of Leyland, GM Buses, Halton, Kelvin Scottish, Mackie of Alloa and Ribble.

Originally conceived with a Leyland Hydracyclic gearbox and a choice of horizontal Leyland or Gardner engines, changes in the fortunes of the Leyland organisation have led to the current standard model having a Cummins L10 engine and a ZF gearbox. Gardner engines are available as an option, and a Volvo power unit has been installed in a left-hand drive underframe and will doubtless ultimately find its way into British examples at some time in the 1990s.

The body has changed little from the original prototypes, although there have been improvements to the interior. Both body and chassis are built at Workington and following experience with the National, whose complex structure generally discouraged overseas buyers, the Lynx was designed with export markets in mind. The body has flat glass throughout, and Leyland will supply underframes to bodybuilders in export markets — but not in the UK, although six did find their way to the Alexander (Belfast) factory in Northern Ireland for operation in the province.

Unlike the National, the Lynx quickly found buyers among small operators as well as large ones. The growing list of Lynx users includes Atlas Bus, Badgerline, The Bee Line, Brighton, Busways, the Caldaire Group, Cardiff, Chesterfield, Cleveland, Colchester, Eastern National, Go-Ahead Northern, Grey Green, Hedingham

Omnibuses, Maidstone Boro'line, Merthyr Tydfil, Moor Dale of Newcastle, Nottingham, Safeguard of Guildford, Smiths Shearings of Wigan, Southampton CityBus, Stevensons of Uttoxeter, West Yorkshire and Western National. The biggest single order for Lynxes has come from West Midlands Travel which in 1989 ordered 150, worth £11 million.

The first challenge to the Lynx proved not to be too serious. Neoplan's SLII single-deck bus was launched at the 1987 Bus & Coach Show and to cater for the British market even had a horizontal Gardner 6HLXCT engine. It was the first European citybus to be marketed in Britain but only one order was announced — for six to be supplied to SUT of Sheffield. SUT is owned by the Neoplan importer . . .

If the Neoplan can be considered stillborn, the next newcomer got off to a much better start. It was the DAF SB220, powered by a horizontal DAF LC 11.6-litre engine linked to a ZF gearbox. The underframe was shown to selected operators in 1987, and this was followed by the announcement in 1988 of an exclusive selling arrangement with Optare, which produced the stylish new Delta body for the model.

The Delta has a strong family resemblance to Optare's successful small buses, the CityPacer and StarRider, and is unusual in being manufactured using aluminium extrusions under licence from Alusuisse. Its competitors

have welded steel frames. The Alusuisse system was first used in the UK in the early 1980s by Wright of Ballymena for its Contour coach bodywork.

The first Delta, a demonstrator, was completed in time for the 1988 Motor Show and it was followed in 1989 by a further demonstrator and production examples for the Northern Bus Co of Dinnington (note the initials, NBC) and Crosville Wales. The first of two for Northern entered service at the end of February and had coach seats and a very high standard of interior finish, designed to put the Delta in a slightly different — and more expensive — class than its other rear-engined competitors.

Renault's PR100 was launched in Britain at the 1988 Motor Show and is a mirror image of the standard French bus, but with bodywork built in Wigan by Northern Counties. Unlike the

Below left:
Interest in single-deck citybuses grew in the mid-1960s. This Leyland Panther with Alexander bodywork was one of a small fleet tried by Glasgow Corporation. *Stewart J. Brown*

Below:
Daimler's Roadliner was one of the great failures among the first generation of rear-engined citybuses. It was unusual in being powered by a compact V-engine; a Cummins V6 or a Perkins V8 were the standard choices. PMT was the biggest operator of the type. *Stewart J. Brown*

Above:
London Transport contributed to and was then caught up in the single-deck euphoria. This Metro-Cammell-bodied Swift illustrates LT's standard design for its fleet of some 1,500 AEC single-deckers.
Stewart J. Brown

Above right:
MCW found a niche in the single-deck market in the early 1970s with its Metro-Scania. Leicester was a major buyer. *Stewart J. Brown*

Lynx and the SB220 which are 1980s' designs, the PR100 went into production in the 1970s, although it wears its age well. Renault claims that there are 15,000 in service worldwide.

The mechanical layout of the PR100 differs from that of the Lynx and SB220 by virtue of using a vertical engine which is inclined at an angle of 45°. The engine is a 9.8-litre Renault unit. Renault uses both ZF and Voith gearboxes in the PR100 which has an unusual tubular steel spaceframe.

The first PR100 to enter passenger-carrying service was Northern Counties' demonstrator, which went into operation with Southampton CityBus for a short period at the end of December 1988. At the same time the first order was announced — a trio of three-door buses for Luton International Airport. The Renault PR100 got off to a slower start than the DAF SB220.

Scania has been selling its single-deck N-series chassis in Britain since 1982, followed by the K-series in 1985 but with few bus customers for either. The new N113, announced in 1988, has a vertical transverse engine and initial sales have largely been of double-deckers. With the announcement of the N113 came the K93, which has a vertical engine in line with the chassis frame. Both models use Scania engines and gearboxes.

Bodywork for Scania's single-deckers has been built by Alexander, East Lancs and Plaxton. East Lancs' styling — if styling is not too strong a word — can best be described as quirky and the Scania/East Lancs combination seems unlikely to win many friends on the basis of its passenger appeal.

The Alexander PS-type body as fitted to the Scania is a vast improvement on the angular P-type from which it has been developed. But it is still less striking than the Lynx, SB220 and PR100. Plaxton, whose first bus body on a Scania was completed in 1989, has adapted its Derwent design, launched on mid-engined high-framed chassis at the end of 1986.

East Lancs single-deck bodies have found their way on to one other city bus chassis, the Dennis Falcon. This was launched as long ago as 1980 — before the Lynx was even thought of — and with a Gardner engine as its standard power unit was devised as a successor to the Bristol RE which had been killed off by Leyland in the desire to increase sales of the National. The Falcon has never achieved high sales volumes, tending to be bought in small numbers by municipal fleets. Annual UK Falcon bus sales in the late 1980s have failed to reach double figures, but the model is still available.

Iveco has been studying the British bus market and would argue that it is already active in it with Iveco-Ford truck-derived minibus chassis, and the low-volume rear-engined 315 coach. For the big bus market it launched a new rear-engined chassis in Europe in 1988, the Turbocity. It has a rear transverse 9.5-litre engine and Iveco plans to sell it with double-deck bodywork too.

In the midst of all this activity MCW announced in 1988 that it would be launching a new single-deck bus, to complement its existing range of double-deckers and midibuses. All was to be revealed at the 1988 Motor Show — but shortly before the Show opened MCW announced that the model had been delayed. Shortly after the Show closed the whole future not only of MCW's single-decker but of the company itself was called into question when its owner, the Laird Group, announced that it was to be sold.

MCW did not reveal details of the specification beyond saying that it would be an 11m long 51-seater. But it was rumoured that it would be a lightweight model with a 5.9-litre Cummins B-series engine and an Allison gearbox. All of which sounds a bit like the GAC.

Remember the GAC? Produced in Ireland, the GAC made a brief appearance in Britain in 1986 in the fleet of United Auto, then still part of NBC — with the initials this time standing for the National Bus Company which was not based in Dinnington. The GAC had a rear-mounted Cummins B-series engine and an Allison gearbox and weighed only 6,400kg unladen — around three tonnes less than the Lynx and its competitors. However, it was only 10m long and a 43-seater. Its fate was sealed when GAC went into receivership and the sole English example was eventually returned whence it came.

Rear-engined low-floor citybuses are widely used throughout Europe. Will the 1990s see them make their mark in Britain? Who dare say? But with over 20,000 double-deckers running on Britain's roads the single-decker city bus has a hard battle ahead.

Below:
The Leyland National was the optimistic outcome of the 1960s enthusiasm for single-deckers. Planned production was 2,000 a year; actual production peaked at 1,000 a year. This is a Cynon Valley example. *Stewart J. Brown*

Bottom:
The Bristol RE was the longest-lived of the first generation of rear-engined single-deckers, finding widespread use with National Bus Company subsidiaries and with municipals too. This one is in Sunderland, a major supporter of the single-deck bus in the 1960s. *Stewart J. Brown*

Right:
The Dennis Falcon has been around since 1980 and sells in small numbers to municipal fleets. Chesterfield runs this East Lancs-bodied model. *Stewart J. Brown*

Below right:
GAC, building in Eire for CIE, hoped to sell to UK operators but went bankrupt before securing any customers. A demonstrator was built for United Automobile. *Peter Rowlands*

'Back-to-Front' Buses in Bristol

The Tilling group's chassis builder, Bristol, was slow in developing a rear-engined double-deck model. As a consequence rear-engined buses were slow in arriving in the Bristol Omnibus Co fleet.
Martin S. Curtis *looks at the types of rear-engined double-decker operated by Bristol Omnibus, which included Atlantcans and Fleetlines as well as the more common VRT.*

The summer of 1963 saw the bus industry continuing to enjoy healthy levels of patronage and, despite growing car ownership, many new buses were constructed to the latest maximum dimensions which permitted increased passenger numbers to be accommodated.

In the West Country, the City and County of Bristol, together with the surrounding counties, werc scrvod by the Bristol Omnibus Co (BOC) which was not only the major provider of local bus and coach scrvices but also, with some 1,300 vchicles, was among the largest of the nationalised Tilling group opcratoro. It followed, therefore, that its fleet was composed predominantly of locally-built Bristol vehicles carrying Eastern Coach Works bodywork and, in double-deck terms, relied on large numbers of Bristol K series and Bristol Lodekkas with either open rear-platforms (for city or town work) or rear-platforms with doors for use on country routes. A growing number of forward entrance FLF and FSF Lodekkas was also appearing in the fleet but these retained the customary halfcab layout with front engine and the driver positioned alongside. Bristol's buses were therefore of a familiar and trusted appearance, which seemed destined to continue indefinitely.

Consequently, passengers were stunned in 1963 by the discovery of a totally unexpected type of vchicle wearing Bristol's Tilling grcen and cream livery — which had apparently been built back-to-front! In fact, the buses attracting this attention — which featured a completely flat front where the entrance was located and a rear engine contained within a protruding cover — were actually 73-seat Weymann-bodied Leyland Atlanteans, which were probably the most unlikely vehicles to join a Tilling operator at this time.

These Atlanteans had started life only a few years earlier with Silver Star Motor Scrvices of Porton Down which was taken over by another Tilling operator, Wilts & Dorset, during June 1963. Like Bristol, Wilts & Dorset was a Bristol/ECW user but it retained a number of Leyland saloons gained from the takeover for its own use, while several ex-Silver Star Leyland ooaohoo were sent to another important Bristol/ ECW operator, Western National. By the end of June however, three Leyland Atlantean PDR1/1 double-deckers (together with a Trojan mini-bus) had been passed to Bristol Omnibus.

Registered TMW 853, VAM 944 and 1013 MW, the Atlanteans became Bristol 7997-9 and apart from their distinctive general appearance, included such unfamiliar features as a

Left:
Bristol's first 'back-to-front' buses arrived in 1963 and were three Leyland Altanteans, including 7998 (VAM 944) seen here entering Marlborough Street Bus Station, Bristol. At the time, the Atlantean was among the most unlikely models to join a Tilling operator.
M. Walker

Bottom:
Two prototype Bristol VRX types were displayed at the 1966 Commercial Motor Show. Of these, HHW 933D carried full Bristol Omnibus livery when new but stands here at BOC's Lawrence Hill Depot in March 1967, carrying Gloucester fleetnames. It was not until 1971 that this bus ran in service for Bristol. *M. Walker*

Leyland O.600 engine, semi-automatic transmission, strip bells and lowbridge bodywork with a side gangway at the rear of the upper deck. Having first seen the revolutionary Bristol Lodekka in 1949, which eliminated the need for side gangways, passengers had not expected to find this item — which was not at all in keeping with the ultra-modern image projected in other respects by this model.

Initially the Atlanteans worked from Weston-super-Mare depot on route 24 between Weston and Bristol, but later moved to Bristol bus station at Marlborough Street where they

became familiar on the 85 group of services to Portishead.

While these buses added considerable interest to the Bristol company, they were clearly out of place in an otherwise highly standardised Bristol/ECW fleet and by September 1964 they had been withdrawn. All passed to Super Coaches of Upminster, which had already acquired a fourth ex-Silver Star Atlantean with coach seating. VAM 944 did return to its former Bristol stamping ground some years later however, when it was used to provide staff transport for Hales Cakes of Clevedon.

At the time 7997-9 were in service with Bristol Omnibus, Bristol Commercial Vehicles had no rear engine double-decker available but, within a year of the Atlanteans' withdrawal, plans were well advanced for a new Bristol/ECW model suitable for double-deck bodywork, powered by a vertical engine at the rear. This was to be the Bristol N-type, a batch of which had been ordered by Bristol Omnibus by June 1966 for delivery under the 1967/68 new vehicle programme, with fleet numbers allocated from 5000 upwards.

By September 1966, the first two bodied prototypes of this model, which by then was described as the Bristol VR, had been completed for display at the Earl's Court Commercial Motor Show. Both had low-floor, lowheight bodies with seating for 80 passengers, a forward mounted radiator resulting in the retention of a front grille, a Bristol/SCG semi-automatic gearbox and Gardner 6LX engine. Unlike the Atlantean however, the engine and gearbox were positioned longitudinally behind the offside rear wheel. At 33ft long, these two prototypes represented the shorter of two possible lengths and were accordingly designated type VRSL (**V**ertical **R**ear engine, **S**hort wheelbase, **L**ow frame).

Of these two buses, the first (registered GGM 431D) appeared at the Commercial Motor Show on ECW's stand wearing Central SMT colours while the second (HHW 933D) was painted in full Bristol Omnibus livery (except that its wheels which were originally black had been repainted cream for the occasion). Both were retained in BCV ownership however and while GGM 431D spent its early years in Scotland with Central, HHW 933D was allocated to Mansfield District rather than Bristol for operational trials.

Vehicles used by Bristol Omnibus for Gloucester city services carried the Gloucester fleetname and coat of arms and this was applied to HHW 933D during early 1967 when it visited the City of Metz in France, which is twinned with Gloucester. Nevertheless, it remained something of a disappointment that this bus was still not used in service with Bristol.

Meanwhile, Bristol's order for 28 VRs was eagerly awaited and, like most production VRs, these were expected to materialise in the form of a new variant known as the VRT, with

Atlantean-style transversely mounted engine, which was rapidly introduced from 1968 alongside the original VR design to offer shorter overall lengths and, more significantly, to conform with the Government's newly-introduced bus grant scheme.

Unfortunately, these too were never to join the Bristol fleet as the company decided to change its new vehicle policy in favour of high capacity Bristol RE single-deckers and at the eleventh hour the 28 VRTs were diverted to Brighton Hove & District (10) and United Automobile Services (18). However, many newly-bodied Bristol-built vehicles passed through BCV's Brislington works prior to delivery and Bristol Omnibus was asked to assist in carrying out some minor modifications to a number of early VRTs. Ironically, this resulted in new VRTs, including some of the very buses originally ordered by the Bristol Omnibus Co, passing through BOC's workshops at Lawrence Hill and Marlborough Street before delivery elsewhere!

BOC's single-deck policy continued unabated until the early 1970s when an order for new double-deckers was again placed and during February 1972 eight new VRT/SL models were received. These were among the first ECW-bodied VRs to carry 70-seat dual-door, centre staircase bodies, the internal layout of which was far from satisfactory. However, externally the traditionally-styled ECW bodywork looked particularly attractive in Bristol's fresh one-man bus livery of cream with Tilling green.

With registrations EHU 361-8K, these first VRTs were numbered C5002-9 (in the number

series first reserved for this type six years earlier!) as the first two positions in this series (C5000/1) had already been allocated to GGM 431D and HHW 933D, the 80-seat prototype VRs of 1966 which, following purchase from Bristol Commercial Vehicles, had entered service as crew-operated buses in 1971. HHW 933D therefore operated in service with Bristol Omnibus almost five years after first appearing in the company's livery.

Use of these prototypes was often limited to peak hour journeys and both vehicles spent lengthy periods out of use until September 1973, when they were withdrawn and sold to Osborne's of Tollesbury.

The entry into service of the first VRTs as OMO buses was also far from smooth, due to a failure to agree with staff on their use on a variety of Bristol city services, until eventually they began work on 23 July 1972, alongside RELL single-deckers, on Routes 22/23 from Muller Road depot.

During the following year, a further batch of 20 dual-door VRT/SLs with Gardner 6LXB

Top:
Bristol VRTs eventually entered service with Bristol in 1972, with the first batch of eight wearing a similar livery to the prototype VRXs. C5006 (EHU 365K) emerges from the service 23 terminus loop at Shirehampton during May 1974. *M. S. Curtis*

Left:
National green livery was applied to four single-door, Series 2 VRT/SLs received in 1975 for use on country routes. Among them was 5502 (HTC 728N), seen shortly after delivery at Lawrence Hill. *M. S. Curtis*

Right:
Roe-bodied Atlantean 8603 (HOR 589E) operates from Uphill in cream livery, on Weston-super-Mare open-top service 100. It was new to King Alfred and later passed to Hants & Dorset, before joining Bristol as an open-topper. *M. S. Curtis*

power units was added to the fleet to expand one-man double-deck operation on Bristol city routes. Numbered C5010-29 (LHW 791-9L/MHW286-96L) the chassis of the first of these was displayed by BCV the previous year, at the Earl's Court Commercial Motor Show.

Although built to a layout similar to the earlier EHU-batch of VRTs, C5010 onwards were instantly recognisable since not only did they feature ECW's new wraparound front design with curved windscreen, but these vehicles also arrived in the comparatively drab NBC green livery with a white waistband and grey wheels. Since Bristol was by this time a subsidiary of the National Bus Company it was compelled to adopt these colours although the Bristol scroll and coat of arms (together with NBC symbol) were retained on these VRTs as Bristol city services remained jointly operated with Bristol Corporation. Rear route number boxes were also fitted to the second batch of VRTs but full use was rarely made of them.

The summer of 1975 saw the arrival of four new single-door VRT/SL6Gs (but still with only 70 seats) which were the first VRTs for use outside Bristol city. Commencing a new fleet number series, 5500-3 (HTC 726 9N) were initially allocated to Weston-super-Mare and were to be the last Series 2 VRs delivered new to the company.

Almost immediately deliveries of more VRTs followed to the revised Series 3 design incorporating an encapsulated engine compartment to reduce noise. Many continued to be powered by the familiar Gardner 6LXB while others

received a new engine option, the Leyland 501 unit. Dual-door versions also appeared outside Bristol city with examples allocated for Gloucester services and BOC's Cheltenham District Traction subsidiary, and whilst NBC green became universally applied by Bristol, appropriate fleetnames were of course carried. Further deliveries of Series 3 VRs then continued steadily until the end of VRT production.

Whilst the VRT could be considered as the standard NBC double-decker, there remained much of interest within the Bristol VR fleet. From the mid-1970s, work began on converting many of the Bristol city VRTs to fully automatic transmission while experiments were also conducted using Daimler Fleetline rear axles in VRTs. A number of exchanges between Bristol and Western National group vehicles also took place in order to broaden the area covered by buses painted in overall advertising liveries.

By 1979, the future of the Weston-super-Mare open-top services was under review and as a result Bristol Omnibus acquired a motley collection of non-standard double-deckers which, with roofs removed, would enable the open top services to be converted to OMO. As a result, Leyland Atlanteans returned to Weston depot as the company purchased four Roe-bodied examples from Hants & Dorset (although only three were prepared for service) which had originally been supplied to King Alfred of Winchester (HOR 589 92E). A further Atlantean with Weymann body (612 UKM) was bought from Maidstone & District while two Daimler Fleetlines from Midland Red, registered LHA 615/23F — which were the first Daimler buses to enter the Bristol fleet — completed the set. They were progressively introduced, initially wearing an ivory livery.

Market Analysis Plan (MAP) network design schemes were being undertaken during this period which achieved, among other things, renewed recognition of the advantages of double-deckers to reduce peak duplication. Bristol had failed to gain any VRTs from the Scottish Bus Group when most were exchanged during the early 1970s with FLFs from NBC fleets, since not only were Bristol's newest FLFs Bristol-engined (SBG required Gardners) but several were also involved in overall advertising contracts. The company accordingly found itself looking for more second-hand rear-engined double-deckers and while VRTs were desirable, very few were readily available.

Among the first additional buses to arrive therefore were three more Daimler Fleetlines, with Northern Counties bodywork (KFC 372-4G) which were no longer required by City

Formerly London Country BT10, 6509 (PPH 470R) displays its distinctive highbridge bodywork with the deep white band between decks, as it approaches Keynsham in 1981. *M. S. Curtis*

VRTs were therefore rapidly transferred to Bristol service and in spite of being of highbridge layout with distinctive deep waistbands, they soon became a familiar part of the local scene, working from Marlborough Street (Bristol) and Bath depots.

And if this were not enough, 1980 also saw yet another unfamiliar rear engine type added to the fleet as Bristol was selected to receive five MCW Metrobuses with Rolls-Royce engines and Voith transmissions (6000-4:DAE 510-4W) which, although intended for Bristol city, were actually allocated to Bath for both city and country work. Each carried a different version of a Faresaver advertising livery when new which made a colourful impact on travellers to whom, it was clear, a new type of bus was being offered for their journey.

Meanwhile, VRT deliveries continued with the final new examples received in 1981. These had fully automatic transmission, the last for country services being powered by non-standard Leyland O.680 engines owing to a Gardner engine shortage. Some were later converted to Gardner 6LXB engines (as were

of Oxford Motor Services. They were again allocated to Weston, which had seen a surprisingly high proportion of the company's rear-engined double-deckers, but problems associated with heavy steering resulted in the early demise of these Fleetlines.

The availability of large numbers of London Transport DMS Fleetlines appeared to offer a solution and several arrived at Lawrence Hill depot. However, although some were painted green by Bristol, all of these moved further west to Western National, as London Country had decided to dispose of its entire batch of 15 ECW-bodied VRTs in 1980 (PPH 461-75R). The

Both open- and closed-top Daimler Fleetlines operated from Weston-super-Mare depot. Surprisingly numbered 7000 in the same series as Bristol FLF Lodekkas, KFC 372G had previously worked for City of Oxford Motor Services. Its bodywork was by Northern Counties. *M. S. Curtis*

many with Leyland 501 engines, including those from London Country). This brought the total number of VRTs bought new by Bristol to 156 with two-door bodywork plus a further 47 with single door bodies.

Nevertheless, by 1983 several further VRTs had been acquired from East Midland, United Auto and West Riding while a batch of 10 two-door, K-registration buses came from Southdown and two convertible open-top VRs were bought from Southern Vectis (UFX 859/60S).

The final new type of rear-engined double decker for Bristol Omnibus first appeared in 1982. This was Bristol Commercial Vehicles' B45 model, which became better known as the Leyland Olympian although most were initially licensed as Bristols. Those for BOC had Roe rather than ECW bodywork and over 40 were in service by September 1983 when the Bristol Omnibus Co was divided into smaller units while, simultaneously, Bristol Commercial Vehicles ceased production — with Olympian assembly transferred elsewhere.

The chapters closed therefore for both this large operator and its main — but by no means only — supplier of 'back-to-front' buses. The events which followed form yet another story.

Odd Men Out

Over the years various new types of coach have been launched in Britain to meet with only limited sales success. Some have been too expensive, others have been of indifferent quality. **Geoff Mills** *illustrates a selection of odd coaches which have sold in small numbers.*

Right:
An unlikely combination for a coach was Dodge and Strachans. Either one would have been odd in 1964, both together were doubly odd. Rickards of Brentford bought six based on the front-engined S305 chassis, giving it the doubtful distinction of running Britain's biggest fleet of Dodge PSVs. The Strachans body was actually quite stylish, with contemporary crispness and some passing resemblance to Duple products of the time. A standard BET curved windscreen was fitted.

Right:
Strachans and Dodge have both vanished from the coach business while MCW is still just active. The Metropolitan of 1967 was a distinctive design which perhaps deserved to do better than it did. It had clean lines and advanced features such as rectangular headlights. Few were sold and MCW quickly reverted to building buses until launching its Metroliner range in 1982. This Metropolitan body was mounted on a Bedford VAM14 chassis for Elm Park Coaches of Romford.

Above:
Another bus bodybuilder which attempted to sell coaches in the mid-1960s was Park Royal. The Royalist was a refreshingly modern looking product, but perhaps suffered from being built on a rear-engined Albion Viking VK43 chassis. Red House of Coventry bought four of the six which were built.

Below:
The AEC Sabre was even less fortunate. It had a rear-mounted V8 engine and was at that time the most powerful coach ever to have been sold in Britain. However, only one was sold — this ECW-bodied 53-seater which was exhibited at the 1971 Commercial Motor Show and joined the fleet of Best of Ealing. Note the absence of any AEC badging in this view at the 1972 Brighton coach rally — British Leyland was going through one of its corporate identity crises.

Above:
Seddon made some slight inroads to the coach market with its front-engined Pennine VI. The rear-engined Pennine V was a much rarer model and one is seen here in the fleet of Coastal of Seaford. This coach was new in 1972 to Beavis of Bussage and has Van Hool bodywork.

Left:
A small number of UTIC Tagus coaches were imported by Moseley, the Midlands dealer, in the early 1970s. These were Portuguese-built integrals with rear-mounted AEC running units. This one, originally GDU 65L in the fleet of Bonas of Coventry, was still operational in 1988 with Linkwise of London.

Left:
Before succeeding with its Bermuda range of bodies in 1980, Belgian coachbuilder Jonckheere made a few sales in the 1970s with its previous Solaire body. This one, mounted on a Ford R226, was bought by Excelsior of Bournemouth but was soon resold to Dickson of Stoke Mandeville, in whose fleet it is seen in 1979.

Below:
In the early 1980s Irizar bodywork from Spain sold in small numbers with the split-level Urko being the most distinctive model. This example was new in 1981 to Thamesmead of London and like most Irizar bodies is mounted on a Volvo chassis. Later Irizar coaches were more conventional in their styling but sold little better in Britain.

Left:
Seddon, having sold large numbers of Pennine VIIs to the Scottish Bus Group, decided to have a go at independent operators with its mid-engined Gardner-powered chassis. Greater Manchester operator Johnsons Coaches was appointed a dealer and ran this Willowbrook-bodied example — but no sales to private operators resulted and Seddon soon abandoned coach chassis production. This combination of chassis and body remained unique.

Below left:
Ayatts of Spain builds striking coaches and in the early 1980s tried unsuccessfully to sell them in Britain. This Apollo has a rear-mounted Magirus Deutz air-cooled engine and a low driving position which allows a row of seats above the driver's head. The underfloor luggage area is reached by a huge single-piece side flap between the wheels. This coach was delivered to Hogg of Boston in 1982.

Top right:
Duple developed an integral coach based on the marriage of their short-lived Caribbean body to a Neoplan N716 underframe with rear-mounted Cummins L10 engine. Despite plans to sell large numbers only one was built. It was sold to Norfolk of Nayland in 1983.

Above right:
Wright of Ballymena has sold a few of its distinctive Contour coach bodies to British operators. Less common in PSV service is its TT bus body, in this case fitted with 40 coach seats and mounted on a 7ft 6in-wide Bedford SB5 chassis. It was built in 1984 for a Jersey operator but was delivered to Myalls of Bassingbourne, Cambridgeshire.

Right:
Drogmoller integrals were marketed briefly in Britain in 1985 but with a price tag of over £100,000 found few takers. This E330 has an unusual sloping waist and floor line, designed to give passengers towards the rear of the coach a better view ahead. It has a rear-mounted Mercedes engine and joined the fleet of Bergland of Watford.

Above:
Scandinavian chassis have made a great impact on the UK coaching business but Scandinavian bodies have not. One builder who tried was Ajokki from Finland, offering this lavishly-equipped high-floor body on Volvo's three-axle B10MT chassis. Castleways of Winchcombe bought this 49-seater in 1985; by 1988 it was running for Yorkshire-based Wharfedale Coaches.

Below:
Willowbrook of Loughborough has a long involvement in coach bodies and produced some distinctive designs in the early 1970s. The 1980s saw the company being reconstituted on a smaller site in its home town of Loughborough and launching the Crusader body. Only small numbers have been sold. This example on Bedford YNV chassis with Silver Service of Darley Dale was built as a demonstrator.

Stewart J. Brown

From Charabanc to Supercoach

Coach design developments did little to really improve facilities for passengers until the late 1970s and the arrival of high-specification coaches from European and British builders. **Stewart J. Brown** *looks back at postwar coach comfort.*

Coach design has made great advances in the last decade, perhaps the greatest advances since the late 1920s when the open charabanc was being displaced by the totally-enclosed touring coach. There have been many other noteworthy advances — the adoption of the diesel engine in the 1930s; the move to underfloor engines in the 1950s; the increase in permitted vehicle length to the present maximum, established 20 years ago, of 12m. But all these changes primarily affected vehicle performance or carrying capacity. It was only in the late 1970s that large numbers of coach operators began to specify features to significantly improve passenger comfort — features such as reclining seats, toilets, serveries and double glazing.

In early postwar Britain there was a vast demand for leisure traffic and coach operators did their best to meet it with prewar vehicles — halfcab Leyland Tigers and AEC Regals mainly fitted with diesel engines, although the oldest vehicles were still petrol-powered.

New additions to their fleets in the late 1940s were outwardly similar: front-engined with halfcab — few passengers would have been able to spot any difference. The postwar Leyland Tiger and AEC Regal models were the most popular, but there were alternatives — Albion, Bristol, Crossley, Daimler, Dennis, Foden, Guy, Maudslay and even Tilling Stevens were all supplying chassis suitable for coach use. The Foden, announced in 1945, was significant in that it had a full-width bonnet with a concealed radiator, anticipating the trend in car design

and managing to look more modern than its contemporaries.

Table 1

In 1948 operators wanting to buy new full-sized (33-seat) coaches had the following list of chassis and bodybuilders from which to choose. The bodybuilder list is not exhaustive:

Chassis:
AEC Regal II
Albion Valkyrie
Bristol L
Crossley SD42
Daimler CVD6
Dennis Lancet III
Foden PVSC
Guy Arab III
Leyland Tiger PS1
Leyland Tiger PS2
Maudslay Marathon III
Tilling Stevens K

Bodies:
Alexander
Associated Coach Builders
Beadle
Beccols
Bellhouse Hartwell
Burlingham
Duple
ECW
Harrington
Plaxton
Portsmouth Aviation

Santus
Scottish Aviation
Thurgood
Trans United
Whitson
Windover
Willowbrook
Yeates

The sale of Bristol and ECW products was restricted to Nationalised operators. In addition BMMO was building C1 coach chassis for its own fleet.

Operators seeking smaller vehicles normally turned to Bedford, buying the ubiquitous OB, but Austin, Commer and Morris Commercial were also producing petrol-engined truck-derived chassis suitable for coach and bus use.

Bodywork was supplied by a wide variety of builders — see the accompanying list which is not exhaustive — including Duple and Plaxton, now Britain's major luxury coach builders. Many of these late 1940s coach builders were short-lived. The market was booming, but when the boom ended, many of the builders turned to other things while some simply disappeared.

However the days of the halfcab coach were numbered — underfloor-engined models were being developed. Underfloor-engined chassis were not new. Leyland had built small numbers in the 1930s and Midland Red, too, had experimented with the idea, and commenced production soon after the war. Tilling Stevens built prototypes before World War 2. But it was not until the end of the 1940s that underfloor-engined models became widely available with

the appearance of new products from Leyland and AEC. Leyland's first was the integral Olympic bus, and this was followed in 1950 by the Royal Tiger chassis for 30ft long bodywork. AEC offered the Regal IV.

These new generation coaches made the old exposed radiator models obsolete overnight. Some operators tried to maintain an image of modernity on front-engined coaches by specifying full-width cabs. This was not in itself new; full fronts had been a minority taste for some years. But now most operators specifying full fronts for vertical-engined models chose designs which hid the radiator. A small number even grafted full fronts on to existing halfcab bodies, in an effort to make their obsolete coaches more attractive to passengers.

Coincidental with the arrival of underfloor-engined chassis there came a relaxation in the regulations governing the maximum length of two-axle single-deckers — up from 27ft 6in to 30ft. This meant an instant increase of four rows of seats — with coach capacities going up from 33 to 41. The new underfloor-engined chassis — from Atkinson, Bristol, Daimler, Dennis, Guy and Sentinel as well as Leyland and AEC — had set back front axles which allowed an entrance in the front overhang. This was ideal for bus operation, but many coach operators opted for centre entrances, which allowed the front seat passengers to have a grandstand view.

Released from the constraints of a radiator and engine at the front, coach builders gave free rein to their imaginations. Alexander, Duple and Leyland built severely attractive coaches.

Burlingham and Bellhouse-Hartwell went for exuberant curves. All achieved some realisation of modernity. Coach passengers were — or ought to have been — impressed.

But the technical advance was all underneath. New engine positions, bigger engines, improved chassis layouts — all were hidden by the new improved exteriors while the facilities for travellers were largely unchanged. Fixed seats on huge cast plinths, plush interiors, wood trim, top-sliding windows and perhaps even a sliding sun roof were still the order of the day.

Above:
Rear entrance coaches were rare after the war. This Park Royal-bodied Leyland Tiger PS1 was operated by Southdown. The heavy full-width canopy did nothing to make it look modern and points towards Park Royal's true forte being bus rather than coach bodies. *Stewart J. Brown*

There were exceptions. Western SMT and Scottish Omnibuses ran large fleets of coaches with toilets on their London services, a feature which dated from before the war. But most coach trips were made at a leisurely pace and included plenty of stops.

Left:
Early postwar coaches looked little different from their prewar counterparts. The Dennis Lancet suffered from a narrow high-set radiator, worthy of a 1930s rather than a 1940s model. But Duple's A-series body — which was also of prewar inspiration — had fine flowing lines. This coach was operated by Western National. *Stewart J. Brown Collection*

Right:
Foden struck a note of modernity with a full-width bonnet and concealed radiator. This coach ended its days on the island of Arran, running for Lennox, the island's major operator in the mid-1960s. *Stewart J. Brown*

Table 2

Compared with 1948 (Table 1) the number of full-sized coach chassis available in 1952 had declined:

Chassis:
- AEC Regal IV
- Atkinson
- Bristol LS
- Daimler Freeline
- Dennis Lancet UF
- Foden PVR
- Guy Arab UF
- Leyland Royal Tiger
- Sentinel SLC6

Front-mounted engines remained for lighter, smaller coaches — most notably Bedford's SB and Commer's Avenger.

The next increase in length, in 1961, added a further four rows of seats: 11m long coaches typically carried 49 passengers compared with 41 in the typical 30ft long 1950s vehicle.

It also coincided with a new generation of mid-engined coaches. The first generation, typified by Leyland's Royal Tiger and AEC's Regal IV, had been heavy machines with big engines — most weighed around the 8 ton mark which was more than contemporary double-deckers. They had quickly been succeeded by new lighter models — the Tiger Cub and Reliance from the two big manufacturers — but by 1960 most operators realised that some of the advantages of lightweight coaches were illusory and new versions of the Reliance, as well as Leyland's new Leopard, struck a compromise between the heavyweights of the early 1950s and the lightweights of the later part of the decade.

Changes to coach body design were taking place too. As the 1950s drew to a close plastic laminates were becoming more widely used for interior trim. Formica was modern and easy to clean. It did not wear badly, nor did it retain odours such as cigarette smoke.

Plaxton had introduced its Panorama design in 1958. This featured large windows and set the standard for the future: it was a milestone in European coach design. Also being developed at this time were forced-air ventilation systems. Air was drawn in through intakes at the front of the body and distributed by pairs of ventilators — 'jet vents' — above the seats. The jet vents were on the lower edge of the luggage racks and could be seen as an attempt to create something of the ambience of an airliner. More practically, they overcame the problem of draughts. Top sliding windows, or windows which could be wound down, created draughts for everyone. Jet vents provided each passenger with his own personal draught.

The first real spur to improve passenger facilities came with the advent of motorways.

Below:
The first underfloor-engined chassis prompted some interesting body designs. One of the more restrained came from Alexander, which built 41-seat centre entrance bodies of this style on Leyland Royal Tiger and Guy Arab UF chassis for Alexanders, Central SMT and Western SMT. However, in terms of passenger facilities they were little different from the front-engined coaches they replaced.
Stewart J. Brown

High-speed running was now possible and two operators were quick to respond. The Birmingham & Midland Motor Omnibus Co (Midland Red) developed its CM5T integral coach for operation between Birmingham and London. The CM5T had 34 seats, a toilet and a BMMO turbocharged engine which could take the coach up to 80mph.

Ribble went to Leyland for a new coach for its London services — the Gay Hostesses. These were Atlanteans with Metro-Cammell bodies offering a high standard of comfort and fitted with a toilet and a servery.

These models predated the 11m length limit. When this came in 1961, most operators opted to run maximum length coaches. AEC produced longer versions of its Reliance; Leyland had an 11m Leopard. Bristol produced the rear-engined RE and Daimler tried with but limited success to gain some coach business with its ill-starred rear-engined Roadliner. Leyland and AEC produced rear-engined chassis too, although the main thrust of sales for these — the Panther and Swift — was in the bus business rather than the more conservative coach market.

Table 3

By 1966 the position on both chassis and body availability had changed dramatically. Full-sized (11m) coach chassis available in 1966 were:

AEC Reliance
Bedford VAL
Bristol RE
Daimler Roadliner
Ford R226
Leyland Leopard

with bodywork by

Alexander
Duple
ECW
Harrington
Plaxton
Willowbrook

The main advantage of rear engines in coaches was reduction of interior noise. However outside the state-owned companies which standardised on the Bristol RE, sales of rear-engined coaches were limited. Independent operators generally stayed with the proven mid-engined layout.

The early 1970s saw the motorway network expand, but there was little progress in coach design. The Reliance, the Leopard and the RE grew to 12m and were joined by the first imported chassis — Volvo's B58 arrived in 1972, followed by DAF's MB in 1975. Imported bodies had started to appear at the end of the 1960s with the arrival in 1968 of Caetano's flamboyant designs. The Moseley group imported Caetano bodywork to offer British operators an alternative to the Plaxton/Duple duopoly, established in the mid-1960s with the disappearance of the last of the other true luxury coach builders — Burlingham and Harrington.

Caetano was followed into Britain in the early 1970s by Belgian builders Van Hool and Jonckheere — the latter soon disappeared again, not returning until the end of the decade.

The increase in maximum length to 12m in 1969 brought not only more passengers per coach, but also more luggage, and this created a problem. The bigger coaches did not have significantly bigger boots.

Problems of inadequate luggage capacity were not new. The half-deck coaches favoured for airport services in the late 1940s had been devised as an answer to the problem, with a cavernous luggage compartment under the rear seating area. Plaxton's Viewmaster, unveiled at the 1976 Commercial Motor Show, used the concept of a raised floor to provide a bigger boot and some luggage space under the floor. It also provided passengers with a better view.

One problem with high-floor coaches was weight. The Leopard on which the first Viewmaster was built was not exactly liberally endowed with power and the added height and weight did nothing for its performance. There were also problems with the ability of the axles and suspension on this and other models to cope

Facing page, bottom:
Harrington's Cavalier body harked back to the late 1950s with its gently curved waistline. But few would deny that it was an attractive coach. This 1964 AEC Reliance was operated by Jones of Aberbeeg.
Stewart J. Brown

Left:
Plaxton's appropriately-named Panorama went through various facelifts, most of which were improvements. The 1964 version still had the crispness of the original concept, as shown by this 11m-long AEC Reliance in the London-based Timpson fleet. *Stewart J. Brown*

Below left:
Some of Duple's designs were strongly influenced by the Panorama as demonstrated by this 1965 Commander body with its slim pillars and large side windows. Duple's grille was bolder, but not unattractive. This Leyland Leopard joined the Midland Red fleet in 1965. It was one of 49 identical coaches and the first for Midland Red on proprietary chassis since the war. *Stewart J. Brown*

Below:
One continental integral which made a brief appearance was the AEC-UTIC from Portugal. This had a rear-mounted AEC engine. Bonas of Coventry bought a pair in 1972. *Stewart J. Brown*

with the added weight; high-floor body designs had to be developed with great care.

The Viewmaster was the forerunner of a range of high-floor bodies both from Plaxton — the Paramount 3500 series — and other builders. Duple produced the Goldliner, a hastily-developed high-floor version of the Dominant, which was followed by the short-lived Caribbean and then the 340. Most of the increasing number of importers taking an interest in the UK market in the late 1970s also offered high-floor bodies.

Around this time a parallel development was taking place — the arrival in the UK of integral coaches from continental Europe. The integral invasion was spearheaded in 1979 by MAN with the angular SR280. This was not the first foreign integral to be sold in Britain. Earlier in the 1970s a small number of AEC-UTICs had been imported from Portugal, while Moseley developed a rear-engined Caetano integral with Bedford running gear, few of which were sold. Scania, which had formed a link with MCW in 1969 to produce the Metro-Scania city bus, used

Top:
In the late 1960s and early 1970s Mercedes-Benz made half-hearted attempts to sell coaches in Britain. World Wide of London bought complete integral O.302s as well as this O.302 underframe with Plaxton bodywork. *Stewart J. Brown*

Left:
DAF coach chassis arrived in the UK in 1975. An early DAF import was this Van Hool-bodied MB200, shown in the demonstration park at the 1976 Commercial Motor Show in the livery of Mitcham Belle. *Stewart J. Brown*

Above:
To overcome problems with inadequate luggage space on 12m-long coaches Plaxton developed the high floor Viewmaster. This one is on a Volvo B58 in the fleet of Tatlock of Radcliffe, one of the instigators of the Viewmaster project. *Stewart J. Brown*

Right:
Despite the general move towards increased comfort some operators stayed with fairly basic vehicles for long-distance services. This Western SMT Seddon Pennine VII in Scottish Citylink colours has an Alexander T-type body. *Stewart J. Brown*

the MCW link to test the market for its high powered CR145 integral. Only one was built, in 1974. Mercedes-Benz had sold small numbers of O.302s in the late 1960s and early 1970s, and even supplied an underframe to Plaxton.

However the MAN was not yet another one-off. MAN was determined to tackle the market seriously. The SR280 had a vertical rear engine and a clear space within the wheelbase for luggage. The engine offered 280bhp (compared with only 170bhp on the contemporary Leopard). And to match the MAN's improved performance there were significant improvements in passenger amenities. The SR280 came with features such as double glazing, toilet, servery, oil-fired heating and reclining seats either as standard or as readily available options — and MAN aimed it squarely at the top end of the market.

Indeed MAN created a market for high-powered high specification coaches. Although MAN's sales volumes were never high — around

30 a year at best — selling prices were higher in Britain than in the rest of Europe, making even low volumes profitable. MAN was followed in 1981 by two other German builders, Setra and Neoplan.

Neoplan's forte was the high-capacity double-decker. The Skyliner, whose design seemed to owe more than a little to 1950s juke boxes, offered around 77 reclining seats and comprehensive facilities and found an instant market in Britain's newly deregulated express coach services. Operators such as Trathens and Stagecoach were quick to see that a coach carrying 77 passengers was a cost-effective way of competing with established National Express services. Spotting a growing market, Van Hool developed an integral double-decker. The Astromega found few buyers after early examples earned a poor reputation for reliability.

National Express investigated articulated coaches but quickly turned to double-deckers — artics could not be used on the outside lane of motorways. MCW developed a home-grown rival to the Neoplan, the Metroliner with unfamiliar Cummins L10 engine, and this was bought by a number of National Bus Company subsidiaries running trunk services on behalf of National Express, primarily to the south west, the northwest, and the northeast. The first Metroliners were over the magic 4m height limit which allows relatively unrestricted operation on mainland Europe. MCW developed a lower model — the 400GT — which appeared in 1986.

Plaxton, too, introduced a double-decker and this used a Neoplan underframe, the Paramount 4000. This was bought by NBC subsidiaries.

The search was now on for both high capacity as well as high quality. Jonckheere developed the P90, a 3.9m high body which had a small lower saloon behind the rear axle and luggage space in the wheelbase. The P90 was built on conventional mid-engined chassis, usually Volvo's B10M. Weight was critical, and later variants were on the three-axle B10MT. The P90 layout was copied by Van Hool with the Astron integral and the Astral body on Volvo B10M chassis.

Jonckheere also pioneered a new quasi-double-decker, the 4m high P99, which was initially built on the rear-engined three-axle DAF SBR underframe and had a passenger saloon in the centre of the lower deck. The passenger entrance was in mid-wheelbase — the driving compartment was in a separate area at the front. The DAF's front axle design precluded the use of a front entrance — there was inadequate clearance for a gangway between the front wheels. (The Neoplan had independent front suspension which overcame this problem.)

Bodies of this layout were developed by Plaxton (the 4000MS) and Berkhoff (the Eclipse) and appeared on Scania's K112TR three-axle underframe as well as on the DAF.

Imported rear-engined integrals were making inroads into the market, helped particularly by the Dutch Bova, which used DAF running units in an attractively-priced coach. Increasing integral sales brought a response from the British manufacturers. Leyland Bus developed its Royal Tiger Doyen; MCW the single-deck Metroliner; and Hestair Duple the Integral 425 — after building a one-off Caribbean integral and producing one batch of Calypso bodies on Bova underframes. The 425 was of interest because Hestair Duple took care to maximise the interior length available for passenger seating by having the driver as far forward as possible. This, coupled with a new seat design, enabled up to 63 seats to be fitted in the 425 — a record for a single-deck coach built to Britain's Construction & Use Regulations. Leyland's Royal Tiger was short-lived. Launched in 1982, it was discontinued in 1988. (It was also briefly offered as an underframe with coachwork by Plaxton and Van Hool. Duple declined to body it, preferring to pursue its own designs.) The single-deck MCW Metroliner found few takers.

It is now 10 years since MAN sold its first SR280. Rising costs forced MAN to withdraw from the market when the SR280 was succeeded

Above:
German manufacturer Setra aimed for the top end of the coach market with an expensive high-quality product. This is a high-floor S215HD operated by Blueline on its service from London to northeast England. Low-floor and double-deck models are available too. *Stewart J. Brown*

Left:
Caetano coach bodies have been selling in Britain for over 20 years. The current model is the Algarve and this 1985 example is mounted on a DAF chassis in the fleet of Jackson of Chorley. Later Algarves have a simplified grille. *Stewart J. Brown*

Left:
Faced with the rising popularity of imported integrals Leyland developed the Royal Tiger Doyen, with rear-mounted Leyland TL11 engine. Early examples were built in Leeds by Roe; later models, including this 1987 coach for Merthyr Tydfil Transport, were manufactured at Workington. A small number of Royal Tiger underframes received Plaxton and Van Hool bodywork. *Stewart J. Brown*

Below:
Hestair Duple pursued the integral market with its distinctive 425, styled by John Worker Design and powered by a choice of DAF or Cummins engines. In 1988 Hestair Duple started exporting left-hand drive 425s to Europe, the first attempt by a UK integral manufacturer to reverse the flow of imports. These two coaches are in the fleet of Hutchinson of Overtown.
Stewart J. Brown

by the SR360 in 1985. After selling underframes bodied by Caetano (one) and Berkhof (two), MAN reappeared in the full-size coach business in 1989 with Jonckheere-bodied 16.290 underframes.

Mercedes-Benz took a serious interest in the British coach business from 1983 after the false starts of the late 1960s and early 1970s and is selling small numbers of expensive O.303s. LAG, which originally provided bodywork on DAF, Leyland and Volvo chassis, now sells only integrals with either DAF or Cummins engines. Renault planned to sell its FR1 integral in the mid-1980s . . . but did not, choosing instead to attack the bus market with the PR100 in 1988.

More recently Eastern European coaches have begun to appear in small numbers. Volvos are being sold with Hungarian Ikarus bodies, and two Yugoslavian coaches are marketed in Britain, the TAZ Dubrava, and Mercedes look-alike FAP FAMOS. The latter is sold as the Ensign Charisma.

Other makers have come and gone with hardly a trace. There are few coaches around with bodywork by Spanish builders Ayatts, Irizar and Unicar. There is one Portuguese-built Camo. There are a few Van Rooyen Odysseys from Holland, and even fewer Ajokkis from Finland. And one solitary Castrosua.

Wrights of Ballymena is selling small numbers of its striking Contour body, designed with help from Bedford's stylists and originally sold on Bedford Y-series chassis. Willowbrook has all but vanished since building a large batch of spectacularly plain coaches for NBC at the start of the decade.

The supply of chassis has settled down. Volvo's mid-engined B10M is Britain's best-selling coach chassis. The Leyland Tiger, now powered by a Cummins L10 engine, has been a British best seller but is being seriously challenged by the Dennis Javelin, offering operators both a mid-mounted engine and luggage space in the wheelbase, and without doubt the most successful product to come out of the Guildford company's factory for many years.

In 1988 Scania's rear-engined K92 and K112 metamorphised into the K93 and K113. Ford and Bedford, best sellers in the late 1970s, vanished in the mid-1980s. Bedford's successor, AWD, has no immediate plans to produce a coach chassis but may do so in the longer term.

The last decade has seen considerable change. Many operators have continued to buy no-frills coaches with a maximum number of fixed seats — and many who invested in high-specification coaches burned their fingers when they found

Bottom left:
MCW had a go at the single-deck coach market with
the rear-engined Cummins-powered Metroliner.
Early examples were decidedly quirky with their flat
fronts and assymetric windscreens. Later models had
more conventional styling but still found few buyers.
This is one of four early models purchased by SBG
companies. *Stewart J. Brown*

Right:
Following the deregulation of express services in
1980 there was a boom in demand for double-deck
coaches. Van Hool introduced its integral 4m high
Astromega. This one was owned by Park's of
Hamilton but is seen running for Stagecoach. The
Astromega was one of the less successful Van Hool
models. *Stewart J. Brown*

Below right:
The first British builder to produce a 4m high coach
in the continental style was Plaxton, whose
Paramount 4000 used a Neoplan N722/3 three-axle
underframe. This South Wales Transport example
has a Gardner 6LYT engine. The Paramount 4000
was later offered on three-axle rear-engined Scania
and DAF underframes. *Stewart J. Brown*

Below:
The Paramount 4000RS was developed as a twin-
deck coach for the three-axle Volvo B10MT chassis.
Two 64-seaters were purchased by Newton of
Dingwall, shortly before the company was taken over
by the Scottish Bus Group. The rear lower saloon,
which can accommodate nine passengers, is clearly
visible in this view in Edinburgh in the summer of
1985. *Stewart J. Brown*

there was not always enough high-quality, high-price tour work around to make their investment worthwhile. But many passengers have benefited from the new generation of both single- and double-deck coaches with reclining seats, double glazing, toilet, servery, TV/video, high-quality sound systems and air suspension.

What next? Anti-lock brakes are available as an option on many top-quality chassis and integrals. Air conditioning is an expensive option specified by a few operators. Sound-systems with individual headsets are available. Three-axle single-deckers — necessary to cope with ever-increasing weight — look like a distinct possibility; there are already a small number about.

Leyland and Volvo, now under common ownership, have between them a 50% share of the coach market with Dennis and DAF vying for second place. LAG, Bova and Duple are the leading integrals. Plaxton is the leading coach bodybuilder and has widened its lead over Duple.

One thing is clear — the variety of coaches available to UK operators is set to continue undiminished.

Below:
Twin-deck coaches not only provided high passenger capacity but also plenty of luggage space between the top of the chassis frame and the underside of the saloon floor. A Van Hool-bodied Volvo B10M of Rennies of Dunfermline illustrates the point.
Stewart J. Brown

Table 4

After the contraction in choice of 1966 (Table 3) there was a wide variety of full-size chassis, bodies and integral coaches available by 1989:

Chassis:	Bodies:
DAF MB	Alexander
DAF SB	Berkhof
Dennis Javelin	Caetano
Leyland Tiger	Duple
MAN 16.290	Ikarus
Scania K93	Irizar
Scania K113	Jonckheere
Volvo B10M	Plaxton
	Van Hool
	Wright

Integrals:
Bova Europa
Duple Integral 425
Ensign Charisma (FAP FAMOS)
LAG Panoramic
MCW Metroliner*
Mercedes Benz O.303
Neoplan*
Setra*
TAZ Dubrava
Van Hool*

Manufacturers marked * were offering both double-deck and single-deck models.

Alan Millar

Operator Influence on Bus Design

*Over the years big bus operating groups
have played a major role in influencing bus
design – not always for the better.*
Alan Millar *looks back over the last few
decades.*

Large operator groups dominated the British
bus industry for over half a century, from
before Road Service Licensing was introduced
in 1931 until its abolition in 1986. They set
the pace at which the industry developed,
using their formidable buying power to determine the success or failure of individual
models and their manufacturers and to determine the level of bus service offered to the
travelling public.

While bus passengers may not have detected
much sign of their being able to exercise much
customer power, the operators clearly func-
tioned in a buyers' market for most of the time.
Their great insights, their hunches and their
foibles held sway and led to many of the
triumphs and catastrophes of bus design over
the years. Their influence went further for the
groups' buying power was so great that their
preferences helped determine what everyone
else could buy.

As that power passes and we await the
emergence of new power bases within the
industry, it is worth reflecting on the effect of
the groups' supremacy: was it good or bad? Did
it foster or stifle innovation? Did it benefit
passengers, operators or manufacturers?
Would events have been shaped better without
it? The answers to some of these questions must
be pure conjecture, but it is indisputable that
these groups — London Transport, the state-
owned company fleets and the larger passenger
transport executives — accounted for around
40,000, or half the total, of the buses and
coaches on Britain's roads 20 years ago.

Different reasons lay behind the formation of
the different groups. London Transport, once
operating about a fifth of Britain's bus fleet, was
effectively the longest established group, the
most accomplished bulk buyer and arguably the
one with most justification for doing so. By the
time the Underground Electric Railways Group
bought the London General Omnibus Co (LGOC)
in 1912, the bus company already had two
years' track record of building buses to its own
exacting specifications at a factory in Walthamstow, North London, and did a great deal to
advance the technology of commercial vehicle
manufacture.

The Walthamstow operation soon became the
Associated Equipment Co (AEC) which moved to
Southall, West London in 1927 and enjoyed a
contract to build all of LGOC's buses until 1929.
It survived proposed sales to Leyland and Ford
to become an independent manufacturer before
the Underground Group was merged into the
publicly-owned London Passenger Transport
Board in 1933. Even then, AEC emerged with a
10-year contract to supply 90% of London
Transport's requirements for buses and parts; it
did not lose its independence until Leyland took
control in 1962. It closed in 1979.

LT inherited LGOC's insatiable pursuit of
vehicular progression and, with AEC, developed
a line of soundly engineered state-of-the-art
buses able not only to withstand the rigours of
traffic in Britain's congested capital, but which
could, with little significant modification, also
work well throughout the country. The 1929
Regent double-decker had matured in 10 years

to become the RT-type with which LT packed its fleet between 1947 and 1954 to the tune of over 4,600 vehicles. Leyland was the preferred supplier for the balance of LT's work, building about half its trolleybus fleet, helping develop rear-engined single-deck buses and, in the immediate postwar period, building over 2,000 Titan PD2 double-deckers to a design matched closely to the specification of the AEC RT.

LT developed an almost military approach to its organisation which, when working well, presented a quality image of dedication to the

provision of a public service. This extended to heavily centralised overhaul and repair facilities which demanded a high degree of component standardisation from chassis and body builders so that buses could be stripped down and rebuilt periodically on a production line basis.

For its immediate postwar purchasing programme, it turned from building its own bodywork to using outside suppliers and Park Royal — owned by AEC's parent ACV group from 1949 — Weymann and Metro-Cammell built the vast majority of the bodies for the AEC and Leyland RT family to a common design capable of being mounted on either chassis.

The provincial version of the RT, the Regent III, was AEC's last really popular double-decker; it enjoyed a strong following from large company operators and from many big city undertakings, notably Liverpool, Leeds and Glasgow Corporations.

LT's quest for its next level of technical progression probably pushed AEC too far. The bus, the Routemaster, was a technical masterpiece. It combined integral construction with lightweight aluminium alloy body construction, independent front suspension and hydraulic braking — all of which were very advanced features when the prototype appeared

in 1954 and were still uncommon when a nine-year production run of over 2,700 buses began in 1958. Its level of standardisation fitted even more into LT's production line overhaul methods, but it was more expensive to build than more conventional vehicles; ACV managed to offset some of this cost by securing the contract to build all production Routemasters at AEC and Park Royal (including 115 for outside customers) and by using some features in other double-deckers in its range.

The Routemaster was also on the verge of obsolescence by the time production began. While LT was pursuing production line efficiency for its overhaul work and was leading AEC into laudable engineering innovations, it was helping develop an otherwise very conventional bus when Leyland, with its rear-engined Atlantean of 1958, was starting to change others' buying plans more radically and was

Below:
A less successful London standard was developed round AEC's rear-engined single-deck chassis in the mid-1960s. This is a 1969 Merlin with bodywork built to Red Arrow specification by Metro-Cammell and fitted with only 25 seats but capable of carrying up to 48 standees. The white window surrounds represented a short-lived attempt to make these unpopular buses look more attractive.
Stewart J. Brown

creating the wherewithal for one-man-operated (OMO) double-deckers to be legalised. A rear-engined Routemaster prototype was built in 1966, but events had taken another course by then.

The industry was showing a temporary, but intense enthusiasm for standee single-deckers and few displayed with such intensity as LT. It placed orders for over 1,500 single-deckers to be delivered over a six-year period in what was intended as a massive reshaping of its route network. Its own technical people appear to have been taken by surprise by this move, so the boot went on to the other foot as AEC largely dictated the design of the buses supplied.

The Merlin and Swift single-deckers supplied between 1966 and 1972 were early products of Leyland's acquisition of the AEC business and represented new technology for manufacturer and operator. They were the first rear-engined buses which LT had bought in such quantity, yet their braking and suspension systems and their conventional body-on-chassis construction was much less advanced than on the Routemaster. The reshaping plan was soon abandoned and the not inconsiderable teething problems with the buses soon persuaded LT to sell the lot at the earliest opportunity. LT may by then have become a less dominant force in the world — its country buses had been transferred to the National Bus Company in 1970 — but it still convinced itself that off the peg buses like the Merlins and Swifts were beneath its dignity or status.

But when it started buying double-deckers again in 1970, it had little choice but to buy off the peg. The Routemaster and its rear-engined FRM derivative were not available, so LT had to desert AEC for the first time since the war and buy another product of the Leyland group — the Daimler Fleetline. It bought over 2,600 in eight years, often starving other operators of supplies as Leyland struggled unsatisfactorily to manage a monopoly of the double-deck market, but was never happy to be buying off the peg and started to sell them as soon as it had rid itself of the last Swifts.

LT engineers spent much of this period designing a side-engined multi-wheeled double-decker, the XRM, and were only persuaded to drop the idea in 1980. There also were plans to refurbish Routemasters and even somewhat fanciful notions of building new ones. Instead, a new generation of off the peg buses eventually found favour. Leyland's Titan, with Routemaster features like hydraulic brakes and independent front suspension, had been developed with substantial LT input. While Leyland would probably have let production problems kill it off at or soon after birth, LT persisted in buying over 1,100 Titans before production ended in 1984. Its purchase of over 1,400 MCW Metrobuses helped assure that model's success, but, like Leyland, MCW was obliged to go on supplying a more sophisticated model to LT than was demanded by other customers.

LT's power over the market was dealt a fatal blow in 1984 when the creation of London Regional Transport hived bus operation off to a subsidiary company, London Buses, which was obliged to bid against allcomers for the right to run its route network. The costly overhauling practices have gone and a significant proportion of the route network has been lost to competitors, leaving London Buses out of the market for big new bus orders and in a weak position to dictate what manufacturers will build for it.

The formation of the National Bus Company (NBC) in 1969 resulted in the largest buying group of them all with a fleet of over 20,000 buses and coaches throughout England and Wales. London Country Bus Services, set up in 1970 to take over LT's country fleet, swelled that total to over 21,000. The LT involvement brought an additional dimension to a company formed out of two distinct groups, the Transport Holding Co's largely ex-Tilling operations which had been under state control for 21 years and the newly nationalised companies acquired from BET in 1968.

Their buying policies could hardly have been more different. The Tilling companies had a long history of buying buses from two in-house sources: Bristol Commercial Vehicles for chassis and Eastern Coach Works (ECW) for bodywork. As Bristol Tramways, the chassis builder had started building buses for its own use in 1908 and soon branched out into general sale; ECW was formed in 1936 to run what had been the bodyworks of the Eastern Counties Omnibus Co. Nationalisation in 1948 restricted the two builders to supplying state transport companies, so the bus fleets were obliged to place all but their most exceptional orders with them. Bristol and ECW also supplied the Scottish Bus Group, British Railways and British Road Services with buses, railbuses and trucks.

It turned out, on the whole, to be a good arrangement, for Bristol was developing its then revolutionary Lodekka, the first true lowheight double-decker with the interior layout of a highbridge bus. Production of these highly useful buses began in 1953 and more than 5,200 were constructed over 15 years; the Transport Holding Co (THC) companies took around four-fifths of them. A range of dependable, if unexciting single-deckers was developed: the underfloor-engined LS of 1950/51 and the MW of 1957 between them netted 3,000 sales; for less arduous work, the lighter front-engined SC4LK and underfloor-engined SU suited requirements.

The Lodekka's non-availability to the open market prompted considerable and often unrewarded effort among private sector manufacturers to produce a comparable bus. It also helped keep one flagging manufacturer — Dennis — in the market as Bristol licensed it to build a version of the Lodekka, the Loline, for general sale. That arrangement did help Dennis develop a forward-entrance version of the Lodekka before Bristol, but only 279 Lolines were built between 1957 and 1967.

Bristol was well placed to re-enter the open market in 1965, when Leyland acquired a 25% stake in Bristol and ECW in a deal which gave THC a 25% stake in Park Royal and Roe, the bodybuilders acquired three years earlier with AEC. The new strength was the RE, a rear-engined single-deck bus and coach devel-

oped three years earlier for THC use and ideally suited to a wider market which was falling headlong for single-deckers. Over 3,000 were built, with production ending in 1982, most going to state companies which used many of them to replace double-deckers.

By 1966, Bristol had built prototype VR double-deckers, rear-engined successors to the trusty Lodekka. They promoted engineering simplicity by having offside longitudinally-mounted engines with simpler drivelines than on the longer established Leyland Atlantean and Daimler Fleetline, but for production the rivals' transverse engine layout was adopted and the model became the VRT when deliveries began in 1968. A lightweight underfloor-engined single-decker, the LH, also appeared in 1968 in the last days of THC.

The policy of the BET companies was less strict, but nonetheless apparent. A central purchasing organisation had been in operation from tramway operating days at the beginning of the century and from the 1920s onwards developed a standard specification for the bodywork fitted to single-deck buses. This culminated in the development of a two-piece double curvature windscreen which became a BET hallmark from 1962 and which soon was used on double-deckers. BET also placed bulk chassis orders, with companies generally buying Leyland and/or AEC products.

Lowheight double-deckers were less of a necessity for BET companies, but the non-availability of the Lodekka did send some companies in a multitude of quests for a next best alternative. Two group operators, North Western and Aldershot & District, took Lolines, others bought AEC's Bridgemaster and Renown or Leyland's Albion Lowlander. But the Atlantean, with sunken upper saloon rear gangway in early versions, and the Fleetline proved to be the most enduring solution. Indeed, BET companies helped establish the Fleetline when Daimler replaced the no longer independent AEC as its main alternative double-deck source in 1963.

Metro-Cammell Weymann, Park Royal/Roe and Alexander were significant bodywork suppliers, with Willowbrook and Marshall supplying quantities of standard specification single-deckers.

There was no great compulsion on BET companies to toe the line on every detail of vehicle ordering, and there was room for radical departure. None was more radical than the Birmingham & Midland Motor Omnibus Co, Midland Red to its friends. Like other pioneers, it had a low opinion of bus design and started to build its own from 1923, complete with its own

Below:
Leyland's Titan was heavily influenced by London Transport's engineers. It was expensive and found few other buyers. This is an early Park Royal-built example. Most Titans were made at Leyland's Workington plant. *Alan Millar Collection*

were built over the next seven years. Two prototype underfloor-engined double-deckers, designated D10, were built in 1960/61, but the company switched to the rear-engined Fleetline from 1963; single-deck production ended in 1970.

It is conceivable that, had Tilling thinking governed BET, Midland Red would have been the principal source of buses for the group. That combination — Tilling and BET — was the National Bus Company's inheritance and there was soon to be an additional dimension of greater moment. Leyland had been developing an advanced specification rear-engined integral single-deck citybus with which it had visions of satisfying the apparently booming home demand for such vehicles and of breaking into export markets. Development of this Commutabus project, as it was first known, began in 1965, soon after the first generation of rear-engined citybuses had been rushed into production and by 1969 production plans were announced.

Government approval of the project was conditional on a new prupose-built factory being built in a relative economic backwater, Workington on the Cumbrian coast. This was to be another joint manufacturing venture, Leyland National, with Leyland and NBC having equal stakes. At the same time, Leyland and NBC shareholdings in the other joint companies were equalised, with Bristol, ECW, Park Royal,

engines which evolved into diesels in the mid-1930s. It also experimented with rear-engined prototypes from 1935, underfloor-engined models from 1941 and was operating the first production underfloor single-deckers in the UK in 1946 when its first home-made S6s went into service. It had advanced to rubber suspension and integral construction when its S14 appeared in 1954 and introduced these features to double-deckers with the D9 of 1958, a sort of Brummie Routemaster of which 345

Roe and, now Leyland National, becoming part of a grouping called Bus Manufacturers Holdings (BMH).

Leyland National prototypes were ready by 1970 and production started late the following year, with hopes of up to 2,000 being built annually. It was a truly advanced vehicle, with structural integrity and easy boarding and alighting features to justify rigorous research and development. It had air suspension, independent at the front, a sophisticated heating and ventilating system and a revolutionary fixed head turbocharged engine. It came to production with the benefit of testing in extremes of global climates, but the lack of operational development was to let it down badly in its first years.

Ultimately, every NBC bus company except Oxford bought Nationals and very quickly alternatives ceased to be permitted by the new group's central buying organisation; even the well-liked RE was off the lists. The return to

Left:
A minority of NBC companies received Atlanteans, including new subsidiary London Country. There were 90 of these Park Royal-bodied 72-seaters delivered in 1972.
Stewart J. Brown

Top:
An SBG-inspired design was the front-engined Ailsa. Western SMT received this Alexander-bodied bus in 1978.
Stewart J. Brown

Right:
NBC's ties with ECW led to the production of one batch of B51 coach bodies. The design, modified from that used on Bristol REs in the early 1970s, was not a great success either structurally or aesthetically. This is a Shamrock & Rambler Leopard. *Stewart J. Brown*

favour of double-deckers in the late 1960s depressed demand for the National from outside NBC and export business never really came good. In its first years, NBC was taking around 500 Nationals a year, but even its support dwindled in later years as it found new roles for double-deckers and, in any case, required far fewer vehicles. The National was developed over the years, with the sophisticated heating becoming an option and the fixed head engine being dropped from 1979. Production trickled to a halt in 1985, by which time close on 8,000 had been built — no mean feat.

As central buying spread, double-deck purchasing was concentrated where possible on the VRT, with 4,474 being built before production ended in 1981. The vast majority went to NBC companies, including former BET fleets. Atlanteans satisfied the needs of a few ex-BET companies and London Country, and for many of these a special version of the standard Park Royal/Roe body was specified with a double-curvature windscreen and lower dash panel first designed for London Country.

Most coaches were Leyland Leopards, and Midland Red's independent spirit persisted with the purchase of Leopard buses into the mid-1970s. For rural bus work, the Bristol LH was first choice, but as vehicle supply became more critical through the 1970s, sizeable orders were also placed with Ford and Bedford.

The products of BMH bodybuilders were taken wherever possible, especially those of ECW which met the lion's share of double-deck bus requirements, plus those for separate single-deck bodywork, and which supplied 155 coach bodies in 1982 on Leyland Leopard and Tiger chassis. While Duple and Plaxton were the main coach body suppliers in other years, Willowbrook retained some of its old BET business by building some coaches up to 1980 and even supplied 50 double-deck bodies on VRTs when ECW was unable to cope in 1977.

The VRT gave way to the Bristol-built Leyland Olympian — a less sophisticated derivative of the Titan — in 1981, with NBC buying bodies from ECW and Roe. But the BMH partnership ended in 1983 when Leyland bought out NBC's interest. Park Royal had already closed in 1980, Bristol closed in 1983, Roe in 1984 and ECW in 1987 as falling production led to a retreat to the Leyland plants at Workington and in Lancashire and the Rover Group sold Leyland Bus to a management consortium which would sell out to Volvo in 1988.

The break with Leyland was not marked by an immediate change of buying policy for, after all, the association with its products and with those of its antecedants had installed considerable

product loyalty in the operating companies. But NBC did place some of its double-deck orders with MCW for Metrobuses and helped MCW break into the coach market by ordering quantities of its three-axle Metroliner double-deckers for National Express and other coach services.

NBC was also innovating on a different scale. By 1985, as it faced privatisation and the threat of open competition, many of the subsidiary companies pioneered the introduction of urban minibuses with orders placed that year for over 1,500 vehicles, mainly Ford Transit and Mercedes-Benz van conversions. Its last group orders, placed in 1987, called for 320 minibuses and midibuses (including 82 of MCW's purpose-designed Metrorider) and 26 coaches, but the group was already on course to oblivion as subsidiaries were sold to private buyers. That process ended in 1988 with the sale of London Country North East, part of what had once been LT's country bus department.

A different, but nonetheless important influence was cast upon the market by the third major grouping, the Scottish Bus Group (SBG), with around 5,000 buses to NBC's 20,000 on formation and 3,000 to NBC's 14,000 in the mid-1980s. It entered state control in 1949 when the Scottish Motor Traction group (SMT) followed the Tilling companies into British Transport Commission ownership. The group's in-house bodybuilding subsidiary, Alexander, was kept in private hands, but built upon the foundation of group business to supply many other British and overseas customers. Today, it has factories at Falkirk and at Mallusk, Northern Ireland and, since ECW's demise, has been the world's most prolific producer of double-deck buses.

Alexander's first expertise was as a single-deck builder and, although SBG gradually switched all of its double-deck contracts there, it has bought far more single-deckers. The distinctive Y-type range, in bus and coach and semi-coach versions on a multiplicity of front-, mid- and rear-engined chassis, was supplied to SBG more than any other customer — from the prototype in 1961 to the end of production in 1982.

SMT, like London Transport, was an early convert to the virtues of the diesel engine in the 1930s and passed a strong engineering tradition on to the state-owned group. Leyland was the principal supplier, with AEC, Bedford and Guy also sharing in its business. For double-deck orders, nationalisation turned Bristol into a major second force supplier in place of AEC and Guy and a fifth of all Lodekkas were supplied new to SBG companies. The VRT would have taken its place had SBG's experience with early production models not been so bad as to prompt their sale to NBC companies in the early 1970s in exchange for 107 late model Lodekkas. In 1965, the Daimler Fleetline ousted Leyland from double-deck business. Leyland's share of single-deck business grew, with SBG companies ultimately buying around 1,800 Leopards from 1960 until production ended in 1982.

SBG worked closely with Leyland to develop two special vehicles in the 1960s. The Albion Lowlander was the first of these. Built by Leyland's Glasgow plant, it was an unfortunate attempt to adapt the Titan PD3 into a lowheight to rival the Lodekka. It was ungainly, unreliable and ultimately unsuccessful with 193 out of a meagre production run of 273 being supplied between 1961 and 1965. With the Lowlander's demise, Leyland lost SBG's double-deck business until the restructure of the British motor industry brought Daimler into British Leyland in 1968.

The other special vehicle was the rear-engined Albion Viking of 1965, a no frills lightweight intended for rural and long distance services. It enjoyed, for want of a better term, five years of production, with SBG taking 222 out of a total production of 239. This was hardly large volume business. Later lightweight orders went to Bristol, Bedford and Ford.

A more inspired development was the introduction of the 12m Alexander M-type motorway coach in 1968, which was one of the first coaches of this length in the UK. The M-type

was developed for overnight London-Scottish services and fitted with American-style sloping windows. The design enjoyed further appeal in 1980 when the same windows were used by Duple in a replacement fleet of Dominant III coaches and Duple defrayed some of the development cost by offering them for general sale.

The experience of the Lowlander, Viking and VRT had a traumatic effect on SBG and it entered the 1970s with a distinct inclination to halt the rate of vehicle development which NBC and LT were encouraging. Not for SBG the rear engine, air suspension and integral construction of the Leyland National, but instead a quest for the ultimate in simplicity in the shape of manual gearboxes, leaf spring suspension and manual steering. Out of this was born another bus to the SBG's own specification: the Seddon Pennine 7.

This was Seddon's last foray into the bus market and, when it appeared in 1973, it was an endeavour to combine the engineering philosophy of the Leopard with the then seemingly unbeatable Gardner engine. Over 500 were built over the next nine years, almost all for SBG. The Dennis Dorchester took the Seddon's place in fulfilling this role before Leyland finally bowed to SBG pressure and offered Gardner engines in Tigers from 1983.

SBG's quest for simplicity also helped develop the Ailsa double-decker, the trend-bucking front-engined model launched against Leyland's double-deck monopoly in 1973. With its VRT nightmare very much in mind, SBG made no secret of what it wanted Volvo to build: a

Left:
For single-deck operation by Tilling companies 'a range of dependable if unexciting' models was developed. An Eastern Counties MW bus in Norwich makes the point.
Alan Millar

halfcab traditional bus like the Lodekka. Volvo knew it would get few other takers for such a bus, so developed the Ailsa with engine, cab and entrance all ahead of the front axle.

For all its encouragement, SBG did not overwhelm Ailsa with orders. It took 192 over the vehicle's 10-year production run, but did not buy some every year. In the early stages, teething problems cooled its enthusiasm and the lack of a lowheight version was an inhibition then.

Gradually, SBG regained interest in progressive designs and bought Leyland Nationals from 1977 to 1980. Multiple sourcing saw double-deck business go to the Olympian, Metrobus, Dennis Dominator and to underfloor-engined double-deckers in the shape of the Volvo Citybus and Leyland's Danish-built Lion. Suddenly, it did not want to be left behind. As it headed for privatisation, it stocked up with fleets of minibuses and over 100 Routemasters imported from London.

The other main buying group, the passenger transport executives (PTEs), is almost as noteworthy for what it might have done than for how it exploited its position as a sector which once had close on 10,000 buses in its ownership. Seven PTEs were formed between 1969 and 1974, responsible for public transport in the major conurbations of West Midlands, Greater Manchester, Merseyside, Tyne & Wear, Strathclyde, West and South Yorkshire. They spoke informally to one another, shared many ideas in common and certainly had interests in common, but did not form themselves into a collective buying group.

Had they done so, this would have made a powerful force pitted in its early days against the British Leyland monopoly. Nevertheless, there were still some major buyers which did a lot to ensure success for manufacturers which did offer alternatives to the Leylands which they all, inevitably, bought in great quantity.

Greater Manchester PTE (SELNEC when formed) began life with 2,500 buses inherited from Manchester Corporation and 10 other municipalities and went on to add around 600 more with the acquisition of the independent Lancashire United, most of NBC's North Western and Wigan Corporation. Lancashire United had financial links with the Northern Counties coachworks at Wigan which, from 1983, was 75% owned by the PTE — the only case of a PTE being directly linked with a manufacturer.

West Midlands, with 2,100 buses when formed out of the Birmingham fleet and the three Black Country municipalities, went on to add another 700 with the acquisition of Coventry's buses and a major chunk of Midland Red.

The others were not nearly so large. Merseyside started with 1,400 Liverpool, Birkenhead and Wallasey buses and later added 200 from Southport and St Helens; West Yorkshire began with 1,400 from Leeds, Bradford, Halifax and Huddersfield; South Yorkshire began with 900 from Sheffield, Rotherham and Doncaster; Strathclyde began as Greater Glasgow with Glasgow Corporation's 1,000 buses; and Tyne & Wear began as Tyneside with only around 400 Newcastle and South Shields buses and later added 175 more from Sunderland.

Government new bus grants helped encourage the PTEs to join the other groups in massive fleet renewal programmes which kept Leyland's factories busy throughout most of the 1970s. All bought quantities of Nationals, all except West Midlands bought Atlanteans and all except Strathclyde got Fleetlines. Merseyside, West Midlands and South Yorkshire bought VRTs.

For the biggest fleets, some of the quantities were daunting. Greater Manchester took 1,225 Atlanteans and 590 Fleetlines over a 12-year period, all with standard specification bodies, 80% of which were built by Northern Counties. West Midlands took just over 1,000 Fleetlines with similar bodies built by MCW and Park Royal; Strathclyde took 800 Alexander-bodied Atlanteans; Merseyside took 755 Atlanteans, mostly with Alexander bodies; and West Yorkshire, from formation in 1974, took 361 Atlanteans and 156 Fleetlines, mostly with standard specification Roe bodies.

When it came to encouraging competition for Leyland, all except West Midlands operated MCW's Anglo-Swedish Metropolitan double-decker and Northern Counties enlisted Greater Manchester, the two Yorkshire PTEs and West Midlands to take prototypes of the rear-engined Foden it developed and then dropped in the mid-1970s. Ailsa scored early successes by selling 53 buses to West Midlands and 62 to South Yorkshire and later sold into Strathclyde, Merseyside and Greater Manchester. West Yorkshire, with Geoffrey Hilditch as its first engineering director, encouraged Dennis to develop its Dominator, but bought none because of Hilditch's departure to Leicester; South Yorkshire, meanwhile, selected the Dennis as its standard bus, taking over 350, one of them an experimental trolleybus.

West Midlands gave greatest encouragement to the locally-built Metrobus, committing itself eventually to producing over 1,100 from launch in 1978 with the prospect of more to follow.

Above:
Most of SBG's single-deckers of the 1960s and 1970s had Alexander's attractive Y-type body. This is an 11m short-bay bus variant on a Ford chassis for Alexander (Northern). *Stewart J. Brown*

takings and Greater Manchester, were cut in size and many of their surplus modern buses flooded on to the second-hand bus market, further depressing already reduced demand for new vehicles.

But is that the end of the power of large groups? Does the future lie instead with smaller groups over whom the diminished number of chassis and bodybuilders and, in some cases, PSV dealers will hold sway? There are signs that groups are reforming.

Thirty-one of the 59 NBC subsidiaries were sold to management buy-out teams. Some of these immediately, or shortly after privatisation, acquired other subsidiaries and bus operators, thus creating new mini-groups. Other subsidiaries went to outside buyers intent on building up their local bus operating interests. From the buy-outs, Badgerline expanded to cover substantial parts of Western England, Devon General expanded into Oxford and East Yorkshire took over West Yorkshire and London Country North East.

Outside buyers included Stagecoach (Hampshire Bus, Cumberland and United Counties); ATL (National Travel East/SUT and Crosville added to its Yelloway operation) and Drawlane (Shamrock & Rambler, London Country South West, Midland Red North and North Western). ATL also imports German Neoplan buses and coaches and has a vested interest in putting them into its fleets. Drawlane is run by Geoffrey Hilditch, who also owns East Lancs Coachbuilders and placed early orders for East Lancs-bodied Dominators for its companies, while Badgerline placed an early order for Volvos. Most of the others have carried forward old habits by taking Leylands.

A further development came with the creation of South East Bus Investments Ltd (SEBIL), a federation of five management-owned companies — Brighton & Hove, Cambus, Eastern Counties, East Kent and Maidstone & District — to provide group-sized spending power for vehicle ordering and for the acquisition of other companies.

These groupings are probably only the beginning. Other management-owned companies will almost certainly be swallowed into the larger groupings; some of the groupings themselves may be merged; and these groupings will be well positioned to buy not only parts of SBG as it is sold, but also municipal company fleets, parts of London Buses and even the PTE company fleets.

For good or bad, the manufacturers could well find themselves back up against powerful, or at least influential, operator groupings before the end of the century. *Plus ca change?*

The PTEs did also encourage Leyland's development of the Titan and there was even a proposal that they join forces with London Transport to build it at one stage. Most placed orders before launch, but the production problems which beset its early days led to only two of them getting any, 15 for Greater Manchester and five for West Midlands. Instead, the simpler Olympian would eventually satisfy the needs of Greater Manchester and West Yorkshire in particular, but it had to share their favour with the Metrobus.

There was other PTE-led innovation. In its early days, Greater Manchester encouraged Seddon to develop its Pennine 4/236 midibus and used one and a converted RU full-size chassis in experiments with battery propulsion; in the 1980s, it prompted Dennis to develop its Domino midibus to replace its Seddons. South Yorkshire pioneered the introduction of articulated buses whilst West Midlands built a guided busway.

These innovations came to an end with the 1986 revolution. The PTE bus fleets remained — for the time being — in public ownership, but as autonomous subsidiaries exposed to competition. Many, especially the Yorkshire under-

Dominant in the Bus Business

Duple's Dominant bus body found a ready market among small operators seeking to take advantage of the Government's New Bus Grant, and among major fleets seeking an alternative to Leyland's highly-standardised National. **Stuart Jones** *looks back at the Dominant bus.*

Launched at the 1974 Earls Court Commercial Motor Show, Duple's new bus body strengthened the then increasingly popular Dominant range. Described in the company's advertising as 'of Phase II Dominant construction, incorporating a square tube steel welded structure', it was destined to outlive not only the rest of the Dominant family, but both variants of the Laser and Caribbean ranges that followed.

The design was flexible. Versions of 10m, 11m and 12m length were initially offered with a width choice of either 7ft 6in or 8ft 2½in. It could be mounted on a wide range of heavyweight and lightweight chassis and met the all-important requirements that determined qualification for the Government's New Bus Grant. From the start it was intended to appeal to export markets in addition to the thriving home market.

Though such statements are always subjective, it was widely thought to have an attractive appearance, a well-balanced purposeful look. Certainly it was a refreshing change from the large numbers of Leyland Nationals entering service at that time. Rather than stress its different appearance Duple emphasised the similarity between the components used in the Dominant bus and the National. In his review of the 1974 Earls Court Commercial Motor Show in *Buses* in November 1974 'Midlander' wondered whether Duple were wise to highlight the near identical windscreens 'in view of the amount of criticism which has been levelled at the interior

windscreen reflection on the National'. The problem cannot have been too great and the screens stayed the same throughout the life of the model except on some export vehicles on which flat glass was substituted.

Buses Scottish columnist, Alan Millar, was more impressed. 'The Duple Dominant bus is a well-conceived design, not only from the outside, but also inside where handrails line the entrance area and only a lack of legroom spoils the good impression.'

A Cleveland Transit bedford YRQ (357) was the first Dominant bus in revenue-earning service with a purchaser. One of a pair, its sister (358) was the 1974 Show exhibit and carried a plaque inside saying so. Both were initially allocated to Saltburn where they worked from the Saltburn Motor Services depot. These and two similar buses purchased later were destined to be drastically rebuilt as shortened 35-seaters by Cleveland, with Plaxton Supreme style fronts being added in the process. All four joined Lancaster City Transport in 1988.

Adverts showing Cleveland 358 in service claimed that 'Dominant success is built on famous names'. Marques listed were Bedford, Ford, Leyland, Volvo, Mercedes-Benz, AEC, DAF, Bristol and Seddon; none were built on either DAF or Seddon chassis. No Mercedes-Benz-mounted buses were built for the home market but the OF1417 chassis was used for export orders. Missing from the list was the Dennis name, somewhat ironic given that both

Dennis and Duple later became part of the Hestair Group. At that time Dennis was not producing buses; it was 1977 before the Dominator was introduced. Duple never did build single-deckers on the Dominator although other builders did — perhaps the idea of a Dominator Dominant was too confusing.

The first Ford Dominant bus was demonstrator JWC 525N which was also at the 1974 Show but on the Ford stand. It toured the country visiting operators and must have been quite a success as R-series Fords were soon entering service in numbers. Morris Newton of Dingwall was a notable customer, taking around 20 of the combination including a single batch of 13. Seating capacities were between 46 and 55 and they were used mainly on contracts to carry oil rig platform construction workers to Nigg in the Scottish Highlands. At the other end of the British Isles Jersey opted for the R1014 in its narrow 7ft 6in wide form.

Less popular as a base for the Dominant bus was the Bristol LH. Some were sold in 1975/76.

Silcox of Pembroke Dock took two 47-seaters and Davies Brothers a 53-seater. Both operators switched to other marques for future Dominant buses, Silcox to Leyland, Davies to Bedford, and most LHs continued to be bodied by Eastern Coach Works. When the National Bus Company placed the single biggest British order for the Dominant bus it was for Ford R1014s, not Bristols.

Operators deciding to go for heavyweight chassis at first chose between two British Leyland products, the Leyland Leopard and the AEC Reliance. Hutchison of Overtown favoured the Reliance for a while, though when that model was discontinued it took Volvo B58, Volvo B10M and Leyland Tiger chassis. Trimdon Motor Services was an enthusiastic Leopard purchaser taking 20 between 1979 and 1981. Tigers followed the Leopards into the TMS fleet, both types seating 55. Graham's Bus Service of Paisley took a pair of PSU3C/4Rs seating 53. On the Graham's vehicles the front nearside seat turned to face inwards and the squab hinged at the base so that it could form a luggage tray in the horizontal position. Among other Leopard Dominant bus purchasers were Howlett of Quorn who took a 66-seater, Safeguard of Guildford which had several, and Hill's of Tredegar. One of the earliest Leopards went to

Above:
**Graham's Bus Service of Paisley
took a number of Dominant
buses including this example
fitted to a refurbished ex-NBC
Leyland Leopard chassis.**
Stewart J. Brown

Right:
**Most NBC Dominant buses were
on lightweight chassis but the
last were on Leyland Tigers,
including this solitary specimen
in Ribble's fleet. Alongside is a
Dominant II coach body on a
Leyland Leopard chassis.**
Stewart J. Brown

Below right:
**The only rear-engined chassis to
receive Dominant bus bodies
were a batch of Dennis Falcons
for Leicester City Transport.**
Stewart J. Brown

Facing page, top:
**Among the smaller Dominant
bus bodies were those mounted
on Dennis Lancet chassis for
Merseyside PTE. They were
31-seaters.** *Stewart J. Brown*

Facing page, bottom:
**The Dominant E was a coach
body shell fitted with bus seats.
This Leyland Leopard had been
new to Paton of Renfrew but
ultimately found its way into
the Midland Scottish fleet.**
Stewart J. Brown

Simmonds of Botesdale, later passing to Squirrels of Hitcham, Suffolk.

A number of operators which had not bought Leopard Dominant buses were tempted by the Tiger, among them Delaine of Bourne which bought four. Fylde's solitary Tiger had 47 coach seats.

It was not until 1980 that the first Volvo Dominant bus took to the road with Hutchison. Whippet was another operator to try the B58 and the Fenstanton firm took a pair of 63-seaters in 1980/81. A1 of Ardrossan bought a B58 with an automatic gearbox which later passed to Wiles of Port Seton. The Dominant bus was to be found united with the Volvo B10M too, and again Hutchison was a major purchaser.

The Government's New Bus Grant enabled operators which would otherwise only have been able to afford second-hand vehicles to buy new ones. Some bought coaches with what became known as bus grant doors but many bought dedicated buses. The overwhelming choice of the independent operator was the Bedford Y series chassis. Many specified two-and-one seating at the rear, giving a seating capacity of 63. York Pullman took two of these high capacity saloons and Golden Miller took another. But not everyone went for maximum capacity. Hedingham & District took five new 47-seaters, Ben Stanley took one and Chambers of Bures had a succession of similar vehicles. Yeoman's Canyon Travel of Hereford had a 50-seat YRQ.

A feature of the Dominant bus was its popularity with a wide spectrum of operators. ECW's single-deck bus bodies were largely limited to public sector companies, Plaxtons (with some exceptions) to the private sector, but Duple managed to attract custom from all sizes of independents, municipals, PTEs and the National Bus Company.

Among the municipals were Chester, Merthyr Tydfil, Rhymney Valley, Lancaster, Fylde and Darlington, all of which took Leylands. More unusually Maidstone Borough Council was an early enthusiast for the Bedford taking several batches, the first of which was widely illustrated in Duple's advertising material at the time.

Leicester's municipal fleet was already heavily committed to Dennis when the decision was made to buy Falcon H chassis. These seven vehicles were unique in being the only rear-engined Dominant buses. Also distinctive was the stepped window line with deeper windows for the first two bays. All seven passed to Thamesdown Transport in 1988.

The PTEs tended not to buy body-on-chassis single-deckers because of the disadvantages of higher floors on city work. West Yorkshire PTE was an exception buying 22 dual-purpose Tiger Dominants in 1983-84 when they were not too happy with the performance of their Leyland Nationals. West Midlands PTE took a pair of Dennis Lancets equipped to carry mobility-impaired passengers. Merseyside PTE also found a specialist use for them, taking 10 dual-purpose 31-seat Dennis Lancets in mid-1983.

NBC buying policy favoured Nationals for all single-deck work but in spite of this NBC companies took no less than 79 Dominant buses on a variety of chassis. Best known is the batch of 50 Ford R1014s bought in 1976. These were shared between South Wales Transport (17), United Counties (10), City of Oxford (eight) Eastern National (five), East Yorkshire (five), and Lincolnshire Road Car (five). All seated 43

Left:
Exports included left-hand drive Fords for Nigeria. These had standard curved windscreens but with a tinted top section, and a polished moulding at waist level. Note also the deep sliding windows and the revised lower front panel. This was designed to give an improved approach angle on unmade roads — but the front step-well looks highly vulnerable for rough road operation. *Duple*

Above right:
Many Dominant buses were built on lightweight chassis. Maidstone Borough Council operated this Y-series Bedford. *Stewart J. Brown*

Right:
A few Dominant buses were fitted with coach seats, as shown on this West Yorkshire PTE Leyland Tiger. Note the additional air intake between the main grille and the registration plate. With only one polished moulding on the side the body looked rather plain. *Duple*

and were equipped with a pram pen. They were poppy red or leaf green depending on the operator, and generally carried the fleetname above the first side window. One of the South Wales Transport (SWT) batch appeared at the 1976 Commercial Motor Show.

In 1980 SWT followed the 17 Fords with 18 Bedford YMQs. Seven were dual-purpose 45-seaters and the remaining 11 were 45-seat buses. It was some years before NBC acquired more Dominant buses. When they arrived they were on heavyweight rather than lightweight chassis in the form of Leyland Tigers. Midland Red North had nine with Ribble taking a solitary example.

The final NBC vehicle perhaps does not count as it was not actually owned by NBC. This was the first Dennis Lancet to be fitted with a Cummins B series engine. Carrying the colours of Northumbria Motor Services it was shown at the 1986 Motor Show in the demonstration park and featured a Thermal Werke convection heating system as used by Duple on export models. The 43-seat bus had room for 12 standees and weighed 6,884kg unladen. It ran for Northumbria for some 18 months.

Perhaps one reason for the variety of operators choosing the Dominant bus was the number of different ways it could be specified. Usually fitted with a single 3ft 8in wide doorway at the front, it could also be built in dual-door layout as chosen by Darlington on its 1976 Leopards or even with three doors as Whyte's did for Heathrow airport work. Mounted on Ford R1114 chassis the Whyte's vehicles were designed for moving large crowds quickly. They

seated 38 on perimeter benches and had the fuel tanks relocated to make way for outward opening power-operated 4ft 6in wide centre doors on each side. It was claimed at the time that the 80 passengers carried could be loaded and unloaded in one-tenth of the time it took on a front entrance 45-seater.

Duple produced scaled-down versions of some of its coach models, at one time building Dominant I coachwork on the Mercedes-Benz 508D van chassis. Not quite as drastic but worthy of mention were two batches of Dominant buses on Leyland Cub CU435 chassis purchased by Scottish operators. These seated 32, but unlike Merseyside PTE's 31-seat Lancets which were big buses in all but length, the Cubs were narrow and had an unfortunate overbodied appearance not helped by three additional grille panels at the front. Lothian bought 17 in 1981 and Central Scottish a pair in 1985.

Recently Duple has offered its Integral 425 design to European operators but exports are nothing new for the company, the Dominant bus having won some sizeable export orders. Sales brochures depict a Leyland Clydesdale Dominant bus for Nigeria, one of a batch of 20, with the first of its two doorways behind the front axle. Nigeria also purchased 30 Ford R-series in 1975 and a further 70 in 1976. These left-hand drive vehicles had heavy-duty bumpers, greater ground clearance than UK models, Dominant I style stainless steel mouldings and UK-type curved windscreens. The 10m-long bodies seated 54 using a two-and-three layout.

Duple listed Oman, Bermuda, Pakistan and Africa as buyers of the Dominant bus body.

Duple's 1980 Dominant bus publicity material usually showed a member of the batch of 10 front-engined Mercedes-Benz OF1417 single-door vehicles for Oman National Transport. These had roof-mounted air conditioning units.

Long-running models usually throw up a few interesting variations and the Dominant bus was no exception. At least five were built to carry mobility-impaired passengers, complete with wheelchair lifts. West Midlands ran its pair of Lancets on Easy Rider services in Coventry. They had centre wheelchair lifts behind outward opening doors and 23 dual-purpose seats. Leicester City Bus bought three largely similar vehicles but had to place the trio in store during 1986 when it lost the tendered Access service to Kinch of Mountsorrel. One was subsequently sold to Kingston-upon-Hull City Transport and the remaining pair were sold to Glamorgan County Council social services department. With the disposal of the Lancets and the seven rear-engined Falcons Leicester rapidly went from having one of the largest municipal Dominant bus fleets to having none.

No Dominant buses were mounted on Scania or MCW chassis so it was perhaps surprising

when Stuart Johnson, the dealer for these two marques ordered several Dominant bus bodies. Though the bodies were new they were mounted on the refurbished Leopard chassis of former NBC vehicles, the original Willowbrook Space-car bodies having been scrapped. Already an enthusiastic Dominant bus owner, Simmonds of Great Gonerby took one, registering it with the Ulster mark YIA 9006 to disguise its age. Another went to Graham's Bus Service of Paisley. As well as several other Dominant buses with their original Leopard and Volvo B58 chassis, Graham's own another Stuart Johnson rebody, but with Plaxton Derwent bodywork.

Disguising Dominant buses by re-registering them has some logic to it when the body is newer than the chassis. I am less sure of the thinking behind the decision of Rover Bus Service in Buckinghamshire to re-register two of its three Dominant buses with dateless numbers. What really confused me is that it is the eldest of the trio which retains its year suffix at the time of writing. For number crunchers Bedford YLQ OJR 338 was previously YBH 368S, Ford R1114 662 JJO was PNM 663W, with the final number being OVV 53R, an ex-United Counties Ford R1014.

Operators chose special features for their vehicle according to operating conditions or personal whims. A popular addition were front and rear heavy duty bumpers. Not listed as an option by Duple, these bumpers did nothing for the vehicle's appearance but may well have saved hours of minor accident damage repair time.

Among those things that were listed as options Duple included a rear luggage locker, three-and-two seating, tint glazed opening roof vents, parcel racks, a luggage pen, and twin line stainless steel exterior mouldings. Graham's of Paisley specified twin rear window wipers on at least one of its Leopards, taking the rear luggage locker and heavy duty bumpers for good measure.

Question: when is a Dominant bus not a Dominant bus?
Answer: when it is a Dominant E-type.

Confused? The Dominant E-type was a Duple Dominant coach body fitted with bus seats. Nottingham had sizeable batches of them on Leopards, Highland Omnibuses and Alexander (Northern) had them on Fords in 1977, and Paton of Renfrew also had some on Leopards which later found their way into Scottish Bus Group fleets Western and Midland.

Question: when is a Dominant bus not a Dominant bus?
Oh no, not that again . . .
Answer: when it is a caravan.

Yes, somebody totally rebuilt a 1975 P-registered Ford R-series to sleep eight with a shower, toilet, eight seats, lounge and dining area, television, video and stereo. In the process they panelled over most of the windows at the rear of the bus. In a February 1988 edition of *Coachmart* a Mr Higgins was asking £4,950 plus VAT for it.

Well, all good stories come to an end and so it was for the Dominant bus. With a final flourish as deregulation came, caused almost entirely by that most faithful Dominant bus fan, Hutchison of Overtown, the Dominant bus faded away in 1987. It was replaced by the Duple 300 series bus and, you have guessed, one of the first customers was Hutchison. The very last Dominant bus was sold in 1987 to Delaine of Bourne on a Tiger, E100 AFW. It was soon joined in 1988 by another Tiger with the new 300 series bus body.

Below:
Hutchison of Overtown was a regular Dominant bus customer. The final examples were on Volvo B10M chassis and were unusual in having stepped waistlines. *Duple*

No doubt there will be an article waiting to be written about the 300 series bus 15 years after its launch . . . but I will bet there will still be some Dominant buses running then too.

Chassis fitted with Dominant Bus Bodies for the UK Market

Front-engined
  Ford R
  Leyland Cub

Mid-engined
  AEC Reliance
  Bedford Y
  Bristol LH
  Dennis Lancet
  Leyland Leopard
  Leyland Tiger
  Volvo B58
  Volvo B10M

Rear-engined
  Dennis Falcon H

Below.
New combinations of chassis and body have to be tilt tested before they can be certified for PSV operation. A Leicester Falcon reaches the required 38°. *Duple*

Public sector UK customers for Dominant Buses

Chester City Transport
Cleveland Transit
Darlington Borough Transport
East Yorkshire
Eastern National
Fylde Borough Transport
Lancaster City Transport
Leicester City Transport
Lincolnshire Road Car Co
Lothian Regional Transport
Maidstone Borough Transport
Merseyside PTE
Merthyr Tydfil Borough Transport
Midland Red North
Northumbria Motor Services
City of Oxford Motor Services
Rhymney Valley
Ribble Motor Services
South Wales Transport
United Counties
West Midlands PTE
West Yorkshire PTE

These Have I Loved

Stephen Morris, *Editor of* Buses, *reflects on some of the buses and coaches he has driven.*

A journalist colleague of mine reckons always to describe his occupation as 'Gentleman Tram Driver'. Nice work if you can get it, I am sure, though perhaps the scope may be just a little limited. I suppose following his example I might describe myself as 'Gentleman Bus Driver', although to do so could be quite a risky business. For a start my best friends — and my worst enemies, come to that — would immediately point out, probably with justification, that I should fall foul of the Trade Descriptions Act. And it might just imply that those who drive real buses with real passengers are perhaps less gentlemanly, which would be untrue and unfair, especially in this new era where the customer is king. Deregulation may have made the service worse, but it has made drivers aware that they must be nice to people (or hadn't you noticed?).

I found out the hard way some years ago that teaching would be a wonderful job were it not for the children. Indeed my brief sortie into the world of the pedagogue had but two redeeming features, viz holidays and the fact that the schools in which I battled it out at the chalk face on teaching practice were conveniently served by Southampton's AEC Regents. So the next best thing to teaching without kids would definitely be driving buses without passengers!

Let it be said from the outset, editing *Buses* does not involve simply spending 8 hours a day cavorting around the countryside in blissfully empty PSVs, sweeping past bus queues with gay abandon. But on the occasions when it has found me in the cab of a PSV it has involved a kaleidoscope of types, ranging from the swift and powerful to Gardner 5LW plodding, from car-like ease to cantankerous impossibility and from the mainstream to the downright odd!

Oddest of the lot, I think, was Shelvoke & Drewry's one-off airport bus, a promising design in which the driver sat several feet above the level of his passengers and which was characterised by a very low centre entrance and flat floor, plus a lack of anywhere for the driver to put his feet, especially the left one which was not called upon to do much for a living thanks to the Allison automatic gearbox. It was also characterised by a most disconcerting lack of retardation when the brake pedal was depressed, which caused me one of my more frightening moments when approaching a roundabout at only moderate speed along the west side of Heathrow Airport.

Over the last few years there have been a surprising number of what one may call odd-balls in the PSV market. Not all of them were bad, though. Almost as far off the mainsteam of things as the S&D was the prototype Ward Dalesman, and yet here was a PSV that I remember with great affection, and would probably qualify for a place in my personal top ten. For years I had taken an interest in the Ward fleet at Lepton, near Huddersfield, as I would often pass its premises on family visits to the wilds of West Yorkshire and take note of this smart-looking blue-painted fleet standing alongside the main Huddersfield-Wakefield road. Thus when one of the Lepton branch of the family informed me that Wards was developing its own chassis with an underfloor Perkins V8 the interest was definitely stimulated. Now my

Right:
The author's only sortie to date behind the wheel of an articulated bus, one of the 100 Volvo B10MLs supplied to Japan in 1985.

Above left:
Former Royal Blue 2365 (HDV 624E), a 1967 Bristol RELH6G owned by Michael Dean takes a break in Buckinghamshire on its way from Surrey to Manchester for the 1988 Trans-Pennine rally. *S. Morris*

Left:
Ramsbottom 17, the Leyland Tiger PS1 which, far from living up to its reputation as a tricky beast, proved to be a delight to drive. *S. Morris*

Above:
A rear view of the unusual Shelvoke & Drewry airport bus.
Above right:
The prototype Perkins-powered Ward Dalesman C11-640, which was a surprisingly creditable machine. *S. Morris*

abiding memory of Perkins engines in PSVs was of an odd clattering noise emitted by such beasts as the ex-London Transport GSs operated by Tillingbourne, and I wondered what could possibly be the attraction of a Perkins engine for a modern coach chassis. It was not long before I tracked down the Ward Dalesman prototype and took it for a spin across the Pennines through Manchester and back again. Certainly the powerful V8-640 was very different from the earlier Perkins I recalled. By contemporary PSV standards it was a fast-revving unit and this fact combined with two more pots than the norm meant it was a surprisingly smooth and refined unit. This was more than emphasised by the ill-fated Dennis Falcons for National Express, which used the same engine, and a more refined PSV has yet to be produced. If only refinement could have been matched by reliability! But I digress. Despite a nicely finished Plaxton body the Ward Dalesman had a delightful home-made atmosphere, with a big Leyland Leopard steering wheel, a steering column which looked a bit as if it had been fashioned from baked bean cans and the longest gear lever I think I have ever seen. Instrumentation looked haphazard too. Yet I was soon to find that the Ward brothers had done their homework and this new chassis was undoubtedly a product of years of operating

experience. For 1981 the lack of power steering was bound to be a stumbling block, yet this modern contrivance without which no self-respecting PSV could possibly be, had been omitted for various good reasons, not least for more predictable handling and to reduce tyre wear.

Admittedly in central Manchester I found a bit more muscle effort than usual was called for, but on the other hand I appreciated its sure-footedness on trans-Pennine roads in foul weather conditions. On the M62 I felt a good deal safer and stress free than I have done in some PSVs with, to my mind, too much power assistance, where in a crosswind one does not always feel to have quite enough control. This is not true of all PSVs with power steering, and from this respect I have always found the power steering on Leyland Leopards to be unbeatable.

The almost universal ZF gearbox on modern coaches can be rather a curate's egg. On some installations it can be tricky business to find the right gears; for all their other virtues earlier Volvos could be quite difficult in the gearbox

department, particularly with that peculiar S-shaped gear lever, designed to help Swedish drivers of OMO B58 and B10M service buses to get in and out of the cab. I was glad when they abandoned it in favour of a straight stick. ZF Leopards and AEC Reliances can be fun, too! But to this day I have not come across an easier ZF gearbox to handle than the one fitted to this Ward Dalesman, and this was enhanced by one of the easiest and smoothest PSV clutches I have come across. The Ward Dalesman had all sorts of other unusual features too, such as a handbrake which applied all four brakes and had a progressive action, so that if anything did happen to the footbrake all was not lost. It was a shame that the Ward manufacturing business died; it certainly was not due to major shortcomings with the chassis, especially after the Ward brothers succumbed to popular trends and fitted it with ZF power steering. I doubt that it would have sold in vast numbers, so as to worry the Volvos and Leylands of this world, but it could have sold enough to provide a regular income for its creators. The reasons for the demise of the company are complex, and no doubt there are many theories as to what went wrong which I do not propose to air here.

That was not the only Ward I was to drive; following the introduction of the coach chassis, which was based broadly on the Seddon Pennine

VI, it produced another Seddon clone, a latter-day Gardner-powered RU known as the GRXI which was built for Darlington and again I felt I ought to have a go on one of these. I was not disappointed; the combination of Gardner 6HLXB and SCG semi-automatic gearbox was found to be a good one and as a service bus it was just as delightful to drive as its predecessor.

Apart from the Shelvoke & Drewry I have found few PSVs which I have driven have been particularly unpleasant. I have always found myself though with a love-hate relationship with Bristols. Probably my most embarrassing performance was with the famous Westcliff-on-Sea prewar Bristol K5G, AJN 825. It had a lot of virtues; steering was light and positive, its vacuum brakes surprisingly good and controls basic but light and easy. The gearchange, with full crash gearbox, was very light but the timing had to be absolutely spot on. Mine was not always. Going up the box was a painstakingly stilted affair, which involved several stops before third was achieved! Once the change from second to third was missed — which it usually was, in my case — the only way to find a gear at all was to stop and start again. As far as changing down was concerned, well . . . Actually I did not tempt fate by trying it! Even in five-cylinder form the Gardner engine has so much torque at low engine speeds that it is possible to get away with accelerating from low speeds in top very smoothly, which is all very well so long as you were not in any hurry. I decided on driving the K that I had all the time in the world, though hill climbing from about 8mph in top was not really to be recommended.

The only Bristols which have given me not a moment's bother have been semi-automatic RE coaches, and again a Plaxton-bodied example with a Leyland engine is well up my list of top ten. No power steering, but who cares as much of the weight is far enough back for it not to be a problem. Actually even without power assistance, steering is a bit on the vague side, and a certain amount of wobble always seems to transmit itself to the wheel. Mechanically a semi-automatic Leyland-engined RE is similar to a Leyland Leopard, so it is surprising that it is a much more sprightly machine, especially on hills. I doubt that the top speed is so high, but personally I never could understand why the Leopard had to be so long-geared. I have never found out the full top speed of a Leopard in full coach trim, as it is impossible to achieve without breaking the law by quite a wide margin; I am told by those less scrupulous that 85mph is not unknown. Surely a top speed in the low 70s would have been more than enough and would have given the Leopard much better gradability, which, along with ride quality and

noise levels, always marred the Leopard and probably keeps it out of my top ten, though not by very much. Also better on the RE are the brakes, which, on those with full air brakes are very good if handled gently. What is noticeable on a Gardner-engined RE is that the accelerator is extremely heavy (and the stories I have heard of how some drivers of REs on Anglo-Scottish services overcame that little problem had better not be repeated) whilst the brake pedal needs just the lightest touch to give a gentle but firm stop. It takes not a little thought, then, to adjust in a split second from the Herculean effort to hold down the accelerator to a lightness of touch on the brake pedal which would do a certain Mr Nureyev proud. Get it wrong and 53 passengers can find themselves compressed into the first 3ft of bus whilst the rear panels can be substantially remodelled by any following traffic!

But it is the Bristol manual gearboxes which cause the most fun. When Bristol introduced the LS it introduced something laughingly known as 'synchromesh'. Now in theory synchromesh does all the clever bits previously left to the driver to synchronise engine and road speed when changing gear. This supposedly eliminates the need to double declutch and means that if changes are made without trying to synchronise them they still go in quietly and without fuss. There is a catch to all this; as it

Left:
42 ATO, the ex-Nottingham Leyland Titan PD2/40 on which the author learnt to drive PSVs. *A. Swain*

Left:
42 ATO, the ex-Nottingham Leyland Titan PD2/40 on which the author learnt to drive PSVs. *A. Swain*

Bottom left:
One of Darlington's Ward Dalesman GRXIs. *S. Morris*

involves all sorts of odd springs and things in the gearbox (which is as technical as I intend to get on the subject) it adds to the weight of the gearchange. A good crash box has an action that is as light as anything to be found even on a modern car, but this virtue is removed with the application of synchromesh to a heavy PSV gearbox. Bristol certainly succeeded with synchromesh in one respect; the weight of the change is increased several fold. Unfortunately its net effect on making silent changes, with or without double declutching, is rather less than minimal. I found this out on a MW with overdrive one day when I was actually carrying passengers. Again it was a roundabout which found me out; previously the MW had behaved impeccably but then it obviously decided I was getting too cocky for my own good and would throw a few little tricks at me. Preparing to accelerate out of the roundabout I found the MW would not go into anything at all. Eventually I ground to a halt and found second, which was met by a standing ovation from my passengers who loved every minute of it!

Bristols, I have found, are like that. They lull you into a false sense of security, and just when you think you have got them licked they throw

another little trick at you from the gearbox department. The main trick lies in the fact that fifth lies outside the gate on an LS or an MW, and involves pushing the stick straight forward from fourth. This in itself is the easiest change on the box, but the entertainment arises when trying to change from fourth to third, as the stick has to be steered carefully around overdrive. Get it stuck up the overdrive slot and you are very soon up the proverbial creek without the requisite means of propulsion. Push it too hard the other way and you hit first, and everyone within earshot (in practice several hundred yards) is aware of the fact.

Manual gearbox REs can be fun, too! Here the problems with fifth are eliminated, as it involves moving forward from fourth into neutral, across a gate against spring pressure and back again. But the rest of the box is as tricky as an MW and for additional delectation and delight it is several yards away from the driver, with the engine several more yards behind that. Here lies my greatest love-hate relationship; get it wrong and the RE demoralises you faster than anything else I have driven. Get it right, and the sense of satisfaction is sufficient to push the RE close to the top of my top ten.

For the 1988 Trans-Pennine rally we took Michael Dean's preserved Royal Blue RE from its home in Leatherhead to Manchester and Harrogate. I could not do a thing right with it, and when Michael Dean offered to take over from me (had his nerves had enough of my Sonata in Several Movements for Unaccompanied Gearbox, I wonder?) I dropped the steering wheel with undue alacrity and retired thankfully to the saloon whence wild horses would not have dragged me for the rest of the day! On arrival at the Manchester Museum of Transport Paul Williams of the GMTS at last contrived to get me into the cab of the museum's ex-Ramsbottom Leyland Tiger PS1, something he had been threatening for years. I had heard such horror stories of PS1s in general and this one in particular that I had so far avoided it. Yet after the RE, despite its advantage of 20 years of extra PSV development over the PS1, it proved to be a dream to drive! It was lively and so long as you did not try to hurry things too much the gearchange was not only as light as a feather but on that occasion at least I could not do a thing wrong. It was an exhilarating and most satisfying run. Funnily enough, it must have restored my confidence or something, because on the return journey two days later I had got the RE tamed too and wild horses would not have dragged me *out* of the driving seat! A Jeckyll & Hyde of a vehicle if ever there was one.

Some makes of vehicle always seem just right. I suppose I have more experience of driving Leylands than anything else, as I learnt on a PD2 and did some part-time driving for a company which ran nothing but Leopards. I have yet to find a Leyland which I disliked, although one ageing Leopard without power steering and whose O.680 engine had been donated to a more worthy cause and substituted by an O.600 which I was given for a lengthy school trip to the wilds of Mid-Wales was not amongst my favourites. This goes for modern Leylands as well as old ones; all seem just right somehow. I once got bored driving a Leyland, when I drove a prototype Olympian around the test track at Leyland. With automatic transmission, power steering etc and no traffic with which to contend there was absolutely nothing to occupy the mind. But in traffic the ease of driving of such vehicles is certainly a plus point. The next Olympian I was to drive was one of Maidstone & District's coaches, and I was astounded at the amount of power it could punch. Acceleration was brisk indeed. Even the latest Leyland product, the Swift, which could be seen as having slightly doubtful parentage compared with a thoroughbred Leyland bus has that same *je ne sais quoi* which marks it as a Leyland to drive and gives it a certain competence not found in other small vehicles. It reminded me a bit of a latter day Tiger Cub when I drove one. An ex-North Western Tiger Cub is probably quite high in my top ten too. This particular bus had a five-speed Albion crash gearbox which was a delight to handle

and the whole thing was characterised by a crisp performance.

AECs have a character all their own, and again I have not come across one that was not good to drive, though I must say I have not driven that many. A particular privilege, I felt, was to drive a London Coaches Routemaster through Central London and whilst in certain respects it was showing its age it was easy to see why the RM is considered in many quarters to be unsurpassed as a London bus. It is just right for the job in so many respects; the power-hydraulic brakes are powerful yet much smoother than air, power steering is still weighty yet not hard work, visibility is superb, performance is sufficiently brisk for London traffic; in short, the ideal London bus. Not as challenging as some I have driven, but then London traffic is enough of a challenge for most people. One of my most enjoyable drives though was in a 1966 ex-East Kent Regent V, belonging to New Enterprise of Tonbridge. It was amongst the most raucous machines I have driven, and was ear-shattering in the cab. It did not help to have a tachograph in the cab, because this was mounted on a slightly makeshift bracket which rattled loudly in sympathy with the all-pervading vibration and racket kicked up by the AV590 engine. The clutch was quite sharp, giving Grand Prix-type starting, and then at a certain point the engine would start to hunt. Refinement was out of the question, but it was a most invigorating drive. The first thing that

struck me, when I finished up on the wrong side of the road on an S-bend, was that the steering was very low geared. This Regent had been fitted for OMO, so there was no rear window in the cab. Thus the representative of New Enterprise who accompanied me yelled something to the effect of forget what you learnt on PSV training, just wind the wheel round! Thereafter I did, though it went against the grain a bit. At least we stayed on the right (ie correct!) side of the road and I was able to keep up with the Regent's rapid progress. The low gearing leads to a smaller steering wheel than usual (especially compared with the massive affairs fitted to Leylands) and light steering. One thing this Regent possessed was a synchromesh gearbox that really worked! It was also almost as light a change as that on a crash box, and had a most positive action. You could get away with single declutching if you

felt like it. This Regent was certainly a bus for the boy racer if ever there was one; it gave you the same sort of feeling you get when driving a Mini; it was sheer, unadulterated fun, totally lacking in refinement and with everything doing precisely what you wanted it to without complaining. For sheer enjoyment GJG 750D has to come at the top of the list!

Also close to the top is a Daimler CVG6 I have driven on more than one occasion. This again is one of the Manchester Museum's vehicles, a 1963 ex-Manchester Corporation bus, No 4632. This is the exact opposite of the Regent V in nearly all respects. It has a typically Daimler character of an unflappably staid old lady. It is by far the quietest halfcab I have driven, and with fluid transmission and usual Daimler quality it must be the most refined halfcab double-deck to cross my path. Its only vice is that it is almost boring in its refinement! The

Right:
Cab design has come a long way in 20 years. The neat cab of the Lynx contrasts starkly with that of the Regent V, though both are almost carlike to drive — in different ways! *S. Morris*

Left:
A good example of the modern school; Sheffield & District 264 (E264 TUB) is a Leyland Lynx with a Gardner 6HLXCT engine and five-speed overdrive ZF automatic transmission. A fast machine, and very easy to drive. *S. Morris*

air-operated preselective gearbox is almost foolproof, and the air brakes are smooth and positive.

It was not intended that this article should become a catalogue of old buses; there are plenty of very competent modern vehicles which have proved very pleasurable to drive. Volvos are usually impressive in most respects, although steering tends to be too light for my personal taste and brakes can be *too* good. Scanias are similar, but the computer-aided synchromesh gearbox can add a touch of the unusual to the proceedings and can be great fun to play with! The first DAF MB200 I drove I found bewildering with its 12-speed gearbox and about three different ways of slowing down. It is interesting though that it is the older types which stick in the mind as individuals, whilst most modern types are extremely competent and tend to merge together a bit in one's mind.

There would definitely be some modern types in my top ten; the Leyland Lynx would be up there; the Volvo B10M Mk III is remarkable as the only left-hand drive vehicle with which I have really come to terms and on the smaller side the MCW Metrorider must take a lot of beating, with only over-keen brakes to mar it. I understand these have been improved since I drove one. The modern Dennis range is usually pretty driveable, too. I tended to prefer the earlier models with flat steering wheels, finding these more comfortable than the later craze for raked wheels. Like other good makes of bus Dennises have a 'feel' all their own which can be discerned whether the vehicle is a Lancet, a Dominator or even one of the National Express Falcons. They feel well-engineered, with most things just in the right place, nicely weighted steering and a solid, reassuring feel to the brakes. If I had to choose a Dennis for my top ten, then it would probably be a Falcon H with Gardner 6HLXB engine and Voith transmission. But then I suppose that is really a modern day Bristol RE, which might explain it!

Roger Kaye

Deregulated Nottinghamshire

Roger Kaye *provides a photographic summary of highlights in Nottinghamshire independent bus operation since the deregulation of local bus services in 1986.*

Above left:
Before 1986 Maun International was involved only in coaches. Since then it has successfully tendered for a number of bus services, most of which it runs with second-hand Bristol REs. The oldest is this one-time Brighton Hove & District RESL with two-door ECW body. It is usually allocated to a Worksop circular service and here it passes under the former Great Central Railway line in the town.

Left:
Kettlewells of Retford won tendered services in its home town in 1986, but lost many of them in 1988. The company is unusual in buying new service buses, including this Scania with East Lancs body seen in Retford Market Place in May 1988. Kettlewell's also run rare East Lancs-bodied Dodge 50-series minibuses.

Top:
Chesterfield Transport moved into Retford in September 1988 after winning contracts in the area. It set up a Retford & District subsidiary with a fleet of second-hand buses including a number of ex-Scottish Bus Group Leyland Leopards with Alexander Y-type bus body. This one, new to Western SMT, is seen in Laxton.

Above:
Along with Kettlewells, Unity Coaches was one of the operators to lose out to Chesterfield's new Retford & District operation. A Unity Leopard/Alexander, new to Central SMT, is seen in Retford on a town service shortly before the contract was transferred to Retford & District.

Above:
School contracts in Retford have lengthened the operational lives of some elderly Lincolnshire Road Car Bristol VRTs. This G-registered bus began life with Western SMT.

Left:
Gash of Newark expanded its operations after deregulation. Additions to the fleet included this ex-Southdown Duple-bodied Leyland Leopard seen in South Muskham on a Retford to Newark journey. The old-established Gash business is now owned by Yorkshire Traction.

Left:
Routemasters were operated in Nottinghamshire by Gash of Newark and Gagg of Bunny. Gagg ran from Keyworth to Nottingham and former London Buses RM790 is seen leaving Nottingham's Broad Marsh in the summer of 1988, still in London red.

Below:
Established coach operator Skill's of Nottingham re-entered local bus operation in 1986 and competed with both Trent and Nottingham City Transport. An empty Caetano-bodied Bedford negotiates Nottingham city centre on a short-lived service to Ripley. The service ceased in 1987.

Above:

Dunn-Line operates this MCW Metrorider on its 600 City Nipper service in Nottingham, linking the central area with the General Hospital.

Left:

Another Dunn-Line operation takes the company on a tendered route from Nottingham to Southwell. An anonymous ex-SBG Leopard leaves Nottingham's dark Victoria bus station on this peak-hour service.

Above right:

Camm's of Nottingham run both double- and single-deckers on local bus services. The double-deckers are Scania-powered MCW Metropolitans, most of which — including this bus — came from Hull City Transport. Camm's livery is mainly orange.

Right:

Mark Kempin Travel operates from Sutton-in-Ashfield to Mansfield on a tendered service using Bristol REs. Initially the fleet included this Park Royal-bodied AEC Reliance, originally one of London Country's RP class Green Line coaches. It is seen approaching Mansfield bus station in September 1987.

Variations on the Routemaster Theme

Basil Hancock *has studied Park Royal's records and found planned variations on the Routemaster theme which never reached production.*

The London Transport-AEC-Park Royal Routemaster is probably the best known, and certainly one of the best loved, bus designs in the world, and has now become a tourist attraction in its own right. The RM was originally designed and developed as a replacement for London's large fleet of trolleybuses, but later also superseded the huge RT, RTL and RTW fleets too. While the basic Routemaster and its derivatives were essentially London Transport vehicles, with only Northern General purchasing any outside the London area, it is ironic that in its later years many operators throughout Britain and abroad, including many of those who refused to buy it when it was being built, have come to appreciate its many virtues, and the RM is now to be found in many places and wearing many liveries undreamt of even five years ago.

It is said that the original Routemaster design included provision for a trolleybus version, but to date no drawings of such a vehicle have come to light. However, a look through the records of Park Royal Vehicles has revealed an interesting set of variations on the Routemaster theme, none of which was ever built. To what extent these were developed as a result of serious enquiries, or were possibly only some tentative proposals for the future, is not known, but all of the designs described and illustrated in this article most certainly existed on paper. The fact that they were all given official Park Royal drawing numbers, and quite obviously took up a considerable part of the draughtsmen's valuable time, must mean that they had at least some official blessing. Three basic types of Routemaster variant were drawn up compris-

ing derivatives of the standard vehicle for other operators, rear-engined double-deckers (FRMs) and rear-engined single-deck buses for London Transport.

Instead of reproducing proper layout drawings of these vehicles, I have tried to show how they would have looked had they actually been built. In nearly all cases this has meant that views of the nearside have resulted because most of the original drawings did not show the offside and I have resisted the temptation to guess at details where they are not shown. Similarly, most drawings did not give an indication of the proposed operator, so only where this is known have I shown a livery of the appropriate period.

In addition, the records of Park Royal Vehicles show a very few additional Routemasters which were actually ordered but were never built, and these are detailed in the text.

Looking firstly at the derivatives of the standard RM, it would appear that during the latter half of 1962, following the use of Routemasters as demonstrators by various operators, feedback indicated the need for some changes to the basic vehicle. Three new versions were proposed, namely Drawing Nos 9344 which showed a 30ft long forward entrance 71-seater (H40/31F), 9378 which showed a 31ft 10in long 82-seater (H47/35F) also with forward entrance, and Drawing No 9382 which showed a 27ft 6in 64 seat (H36/28R) rear entrance bus. The last was virtually identical to the standard LT bus and the first was broadly similar to the batch built for Northern General and of course LT's own RMF 1254. The 82-seater had the same basic layout as the RMF

but with an elongated rearmost bay, giving a rear overhang of 9ft 6in which was exceptionally long for the time. All three designs were unmistakably Routemasters, but had features such as sliding instead of wind-down windows for ventilation, fixed front upper deck windows, and additional ventilators in the front roof dome, though no doubt any of these features could have been altered to suit individual operators' requirements. No details of the interiors were shown apart from seating layouts, but it is probable that the interior trim would have been different in order to reduce costs. Mechanically all the variants were based on the RM6 model.

The FRM is one of the great might have beens of the postwar UK bus story, and Park Royal obviously had a good look at the idea. Drawing No 9472 was dated July 1964 and must have been made at about the same time as the first proper proposals were being put together at Chiswick. It showed a rear-engined double-decker which bore an obvious resemblance to what eventually became FRM 1, but with a shorter rear overhang and a more conventional treatment of the engine bustle. In fact, as drawn it had an Atlantean engine cover, probably because the draughtsman knew of little else! The layout showed a 72-seater (H39/33F), and the scheme differed from the FRM in the use of

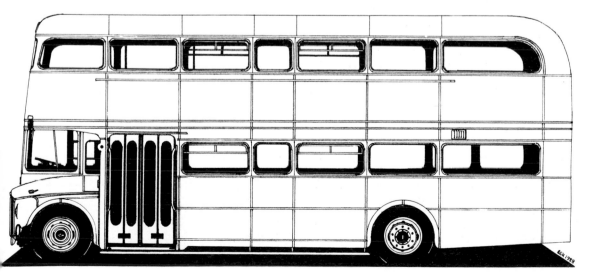

conventional ventilation, with opening windows, and a front end using flat windscreens
and different lower panels, apparently owing a
lot to the Atlantean and Fleetline body design
then being built by Park Royal for Sheffield,
amongst others.

By the time that Drawing No 9520 was made
in September 1965, the layout of the FRM was
obviously more advanced, and this drawing
showed the details of the 'Provincial FRM
Standard', to quote from its official title. The bus
looked much more like the FRM, even down to
its seating layout (H41/31F) and the use of fixed
windows and a forced-air ventilation system.
The major areas of difference were in the use of
only a single front destination/route number

box and, most notably, in the use of double curvature BET windscreens together with a redesigned curved lower front, which added 8in to the overall length. The interior layout was notable for its apparent use of filament rather than fluorescent lighting.

By this time, enthusiasm for the Routemaster must have been running high at Park Royal Vehicles, for the company then went on to produce two layouts for 36ft-long rear-engined single-deck Routemasters. The first, Drawing No 9498 of March 1965, showed a single door vehicle with a body style broadly similar to contemporary BET single-deckers, though with rather flatter windscreens. Some 45 seats were to be fitted, and the relatively low floor height allowed the overall height to be as low as 9ft 2in. The most notable feature of the body's appearance was the use of curved rear corner windows, raked back in Ford Anglia style, with a recessed centre portion to allow for the engine cover to be opened, which led to a very short rear engine bustle. Mechanically the bus was described as being mounted on a 'rear engine chassis — LTB type — RMR running units'. Was it possible that the FRM too was originally to have been the RMR?

Five months later a modified version, Drawing No 9516, appeared, and this time the vehicle was a two-door (front entrance, centre exit) 43-seater mounted on FRM running units. The front overhang had been extended by 6in, and the wheelbase shortened by a similar amount,

while the rear end styling had been tidied up to a modified BET style, although still retaining the recess for opening the engine cover. The use of a rear overhang of no less than 10ft 6in in combination with a wheelbase of only 18ft, together with a transverse power pack mounted at the extreme rear and a very low height body can be expected to have led to some body problems later in life, not to mention making for a choppy ride, while the very low height at which the engine was mounted could have caused frequent problems with the rear end grounding. Certainly it has to be said that not a lot of detailed thinking appears to have gone into these two proposals, and it was probably as well from the point of view of the Routemaster's reputation that these two single-deck variants were never built.

So much for the designs that were drawn up, but what about the Routemasters that were never built? Park Royal Vehicles used to issue a periodic internal document detailing vehicles on order and 'on hand' (ie in course of construction), and in December 1962 a new vehicle appeared on this list. Body No B49807 was described as a '78-seater forward entrance double-deck omnibus incorporating AEC running units, 31ft 8in by 8ft'. While not actually described as a Routemaster, the use of AEC running units rather than a chassis implies that it was a Routemaster since the only other likely contender, the Bridgemaster, was by then out of production. However the length was greater than normal for the time but the details as shown match almost exactly the extended overhang RMF detailed on Drawing No 9378, except for having 78 seats rather than 82. But, for whatever reason, B49807 did not materialise and despite being shown as on hand until 28 December 1963 had disappeared by 28 April 1964, when the next 'on hand' list appeared.

Coincidentally, also in April 1964 there appeared the first mention of body Nos B53296-53298 'Front entrance RM double deck demonstrator' and here we have possibly the first evidence not only of the FRM but also of the fact that there were actually three such vehicles ordered. All three vehicles then appeared regularly in the lists until 31 December 1965 when the order was reduced to B53296 only, with B53297 and B53298 cancelled. B53296 then continued to appear in the 'on hand' listings until 2 April 1966, but had disappeared by 2 July 1966, at about the same time as the first sightings of FRM 1 were made at Chiswick.

B53296 was FRM 1, but what happened to the other two FRMs, and how much, if any, of them was actually built, remains to be seen. However there were very strong rumours at the time that a demonstrator was to have appeared, probably at the 1966 Commercial Motor Show, in Sheffield livery (probably for the A, or Corporation-owned, fleet) and it is likely that Drawing No 9520 described above shows such a vehicle, which was presumably to have been either B53297 or B53298.

Surprisingly, the FRM story does not end there as in March 1965 B54147 was ordered as one 'set of pattern parts of front entrance RM double-deck vehicles B53296-53298', and this was listed as 'on hand' from then until 31 December 1966, but had gone by 1 April 1967. No other information is given, but it

seems most curious that another set of FRM parts was apparently constructed after the cancellation of the other two vehicles. Was this perhaps just a set of spare components for FRM 1, or does the phrase 'pattern parts' imply that they were made to enable the setting up of a production line? Unfortunately the Park Royal records are silent on that one.

Perhaps the most odd thing about the five vehicles mentioned above is that not only were they all actually ordered, but that those that never materialised survived in the 'on hand' listings for as long as they did (a minimum of 12 months for B49807, 19 months for B53297/8, and 21 months for B54147). The questions must be asked as to why they were apparently being built as firm orders for so long, how much manufacture, if any, was carried out on them, why they never appeared, and what became of them. The answers have yet to be found.

This article only concentrates on the Park Royal drawings and orders, but it is interesting to speculate on what other Routemaster designs might have been drawn up by AEC and by London Transport itself. And, of course, there were two other Routemaster derivatives. The Leyland B15, later known as the Titan, originally started out as a double-deck bus based on FRM-type units, to use its official original description, though it certainly deviated from that initial intention, and London Transport itself spent many years working on all sorts of advanced double-deckers under the overall project name of the XRM. However neither the Titan nor the XRM can really be said to have been close Routemaster derivatives, even if the RM provided the original inspiration.

Left:
Park Royal Drawing No 9520 showing 77-passenger front entrance rear engine integral double-deck bus, provincial FRM standard, 14 September 1965.

Anglo-Scottish Coaching

The Scottish Bus Group of companies has tended to follow an individualistic line in the purchase of coaches for long distance express services. The Group's prestigious Anglo-Scottish routes have in recent years been operated by a wide variety of coaches as illustrated by **Kevin Lane**.

Left:
Alexander's 12m-long M-type body was developed for the Scottish Bus Group's London services and offered a standard of comfort which was considerably ahead of its time. The early examples were on 12m Bristol REMH6G chassis and had double glazing, reclining seats, toilet and oil-fired auxiliary heating. A Western Scottish Bristol in corporate blue and white London service livery leaves Grantham for Glasgow in 1982.

Below:
Later M-types were on Volvo B58, Leyland Leopard and — a most unlikely combination — Seddon Pennine VII chassis. A Western Volvo B58 leaves London Victoria in 1981.

Right:
Most Seddon coaches for the Scottish Bus Group had Alexander T-type bodies. A pair of black and white-liveried Western SMT Pennine VIIs leave Dunstable in the summer of 1980 on the weekend 926 service to Glasgow operated jointly with Premier Travel of Cambridge. These were 11m long coaches with Gardner 6HLXB engines, 49 fixed seats and no toilets.

Below:
Replacements for the M-types were built by Duple which developed the Dominant III and a version of the high-floor Goldliner with sloping window frames. This was an early Leyland Tiger, new to Eastern Scottish, and subsequently operated by Midland, before passing to the new Kelvin company in 1985. It is seen here in Kelvin ownership, despite the fleetname on the front, and in the two-tone blue and yellow Citylink livery adopted for express coaches in 1983.

Left:
The Goldliners were initially operated in blue and white as seen on this Northern Tiger passing through Darlington on its way from Dundee to Rugby in 1985.

Below:
Among the more unusual coaches in Citylink colours are four Berkhof-bodied Volvo B10Ms in the Western fleet. Three are twin-deck Emperors, including this 60-seater seen in Finchley Road, London, in 1988. It sports a modified Citylink livery with large fleetname on the side and a Western Scottish name on the front inspired by the style devised by Western SMT in the 1930s.

Above:
Most SBG companies favoured Duple bodywork for Tiger coaches, including Midland, which took this Laser 2 in 1985. It is seen in Llandudno when new, alongside an ageing Crosville Plaxton-bodied Bristol RELH which was providing duplication as far a Liverpool.

Left:
More recently the Hestair Duple 340 has been chosen. This is a Central Scottish Tiger, one of five with Leyland TL11H engines delivered in 1986. It is seen loading at Heathrow Airport for Glasgow in September 1988.

Right:
Tailpiece: a Midland Tiger/Laser loads at Sheffield. Note the toilet compartment in the rear nearside corner.

Close Enough for Jazz

For those of us who aspire to run our own buses but lack the space or the cash for the real thing **Gavin Booth** *takes a look at diecast alternatives.*

The first bus fleet I ever owned was a fairly mixed one. There were a few Duple Roadmaster-bodied Leyland Royal Tigers, some halfcab Guy Arabs, a Harrington Contender, a couple of elderly double-deckers and a handful of Maudslays — some with deck-and-a-half bodywork. A typical bus fleet of the 1950s, as those of you with long memories will readily acknowledge.

Or rather — a typical Dinky Toys bus fleet of the 1950s, a fleet that successfully avoided any resemblance to any other in Britain, with faithful diecast replicas of real bus and coach models that in some cases barely got into double figures. But it is fair to say that 30 years of increasing sophistication and market awareness has gone some way towards alerting the toymakers that the real buses out there on the streets were nothing like the ones they chose to replicate — even if today they still manage to get things wrong.

My solution in the 1950s was simple: a file, some plasticine and a tin of Woolworth's paint. With these essential tools I converted Dinky double-deckers based on prewar London designs into something more modern. I filed off the roof number boxes, encased the bonnets, radiators and wings in plasticine, and even enclosed rear platforms to produce supposedly 'modern' forward entrance double-deckers. Needless to say, the results were pretty awful, but in your pre-teenage years, you tend to be easily satisfied.

The conversions on single-deckers were less dramatic. The Duple Roadmaster Royal Tiger became a more modern single-deck bus with thin layers of plasticine to deepen the roof line and to hide the prominent body mouldings. There really was not much you could do with a deck-and-a-half Maudslay, even by using plasticine.

Dinky Toys Buses and Coaches

This list details all the bus and coach models produced by Dinky Toys, showing the date first introduced, the date finally withdrawn from the catalogue, and the scale. It does not take into account livery variations using the same casting.

1934	Motor Bus (AEC Q)	1939	1/125
1936	Streamline Bus	1950	1/90
1938	Double-Decker Motor Bus (STL)	1963	1/76
1948	Single-Deck Bus (Duple halfcab)	1952	1/76
1950	Observation Coach (Deck-and-a-half)	1960	1/76
1951	Luxury Coach (Maudslay/Duple)	1959	1/76
1952	Duple Roadmaster Coach	1960	1/76
1956	BOAC Coach (Harrington Contender)	1963	1/76
1961	Wayne School Bus	1965	1/56
1963	Atlantean Bus	1968	1/75
1964	Vega Major Luxury Coach (Bedford VAL)	1977	1/45
1964	Routemaster London Bus	1979	1/69
1971	Single-Decker Bus (AEC Red Arrow)	1976	1/64
1972	Luxury Coach (Viceroy 37)	1978	1/95
1973	Atlantean City Bus (SELNEC-type)	1978	1/76

My fleet was painted in Woolworth's Pillar Box Red and White, with the fleetname FORTH carefully applied in Indian ink. The same ink created forward entrance, extra destination screens, and could help make windows look bigger.

At the time I was happy. My smart red-painted fleet now comprised up-to-date models which Dinky Toys in its wisdom had chosen to ignore. The fact that I was defiling models that today would be worth considerable sums never entered my mind. Even my Trojan Van 'Oxo', now apparently a 'very scarce' and therefore valuable item, became Forth's traffic patrol vehicle — after all, my local municipality ran such vans.

In this article I am particularly concerned with the mainstream diecast models to roughly OO scale; white metal kits have always seemed too much like hard work, and the smaller-scale models are worth an article of their own.

For many years Dinky persevered with the same range of buses and coaches. The famous 29c model of 1938, clearly based on prewar London Transport STL class buses, was the only double-deck Dinky from its reintroduction after the war until 1963, albeit in various colour schemes and with radiators apparently representing AEC or Leyland, subject presumably to the whim of someone at Binns Road. The

Top:
Lledo's smaller-scale Models of Days Gone range have worn a bewildering array of liveries, including a few that were actually appropriate. The photograph demonstrates the difference in scale between the two AECs on the left and the normal control bus on the right. *Stewart J. Brown*

Below:
Four staple Dinky products that were on the market together in the late 1950s: the 'luxury coach', the 'observation coach', the Duple Roadmaster and the BOAC Harrington Contender. *Stewart J. Brown*

ultimate 29c was the all-red version (now renumbered 291) of 1959, probably an attempt at a London bus, when an RT or even a Routemaster would have been infinitely more acceptable. It was left to Solido to produce its larger-scale RT model some years later.

The original prewar Dinky range had included a double-deck AEC Q model from 1934 until 1939, hardly a typical bus, but unquestionably modern. And there was a strange single-deck 'streamline bus' that was also sold after the war; while it was not a wonderful model, you could see why its modern lines attracted the men at Meccano.

A more typical Dinky coach model appeared in 1948, the 'single-deck bus', actually a halfcab coach that was based on postwar Duple designs, with the swept waistline and side flashes of the time. Like the 29c double-decker it was known to sport various radiator styles. It suffered the fate of premature obsolescence that dogged many of the real vehicles — overtaken by the appearance of underfloor-engined single-deckers — and was in the Dinky range only until 1952.

The fashion for full-fronted coaches may have prompted Dinky to introduce the 'observation coach' in 1950, a deck-and-a-half body, probably modelled on a Whitson design, on a Maudslay Marathon III chassis — a combination that may never have existed in real life. Such coaches were most commonly built for airport work, providing a sizeable luggage area under the rear raised portion. This model was followed in 1951 by the 'luxury coach', apparently a Duple body, but again with the Maudslay radiator.

When the underfloor-engined single-deckers came along, Dinky appear to have contacted their friends at Duple, who produced drawings of the new Roadmaster coach body. This was never a best seller as a full-size coach. It was metal-framed, when most coach bodies were still wood-framed, and it had a straight, almost austere, waistline, when the fashion was for garish sweeps and swoops. While hindsight tells us that a Burlingham Seagull would have been a better bet for Dinky, the Roadmaster enjoyed great success between 1952 and 1960 — in $1/76$th scale at least.

Dinky got it wrong again in 1956 with its next bus model. This was the first Dinky bus to carry a *real* livery and in place of the usual

anonymity the new coach was in the dark blue and white of the British Overseas Airways Corporation. So far so good. But instead of a typical coach of the time — maybe a Duple Elizabethan or a Plaxton Venturer — it was a Harrington Contender, a rare integral vehicle using the Commer TS3 engine.

I cannot help feeling that real bus operators at that time would have been well advised to watch closely the models chosen for the Dinky range, as a clear indication of what *not* to buy.

Dinky's next bus was also not the first bus in the larger Supertoys range. Sadly it was far from representative of anything British (or even American) — a Wayne school bus. The larger scale allowed better detailing, and no doubt Dinky had transatlantic sales ambitions, but the Wayne was a disappointing addition for most British collectors. The Wayne was on the model market from 1961 to 1964, and in 1963 was joined by a reliveried version, rather unconvincingly lettered Dinky Continental Tours, and described as a 'Continental Touring Coach' Although it was one of the least appropriate Dinkys of the period, if you have one that is still in good condition it is now worth more than £200, according to the authoritative bi-monthly magazine *Model Collector*.

The situation improved in the early 1960s when Dinky actually managed to produce models of buses that could be seen in reasonable

quantities on Britain's streets. First was a Leyland Atlantean in 1962, then followed a Routemaster and a Bedford VAL in 1964.

On the streets, the Atlantean had been around in growing numbers since the end of 1958. The model represented was based on the MCW bodywork fitted to many early Atlanteans, in that it was not very attractive. It did, however, *look* like buses running in many British towns and cities.

The Atlantean was first introduced in red and cream with Ribble or 'Corporation Transport' fleetnames. Ribble was an early Atlantean user, and while the livery was not accurate, it was a sensible move. In 1963 a green and white 'Corporation Transport' version appeared. The Dinky Atlantean lives on in left-hand drive form in Portugal, where the Metosul Autocarro 2 Pisos in a variety of Portuguese liveries was still on sale in Lisbon in 1988 for the equivalent of less than £2.

The choice of the Routemaster was a safe one. When the Dinky Routemaster replaced the old faithful STL in 1964 there were already about 2,000 RMs on the streets of London. The model was good, but disappointing in some of the detail treatment of the front end.

Bedford's twin-steer VAL model was one of the sensations of the 1962 Commercial Motor Show, and many examples carried Duple Super Vega bodywork, so the Dinky Supertoys (1/45th scale) model that appeared in 1964 was an accurate reproduction of a familiar coach model. Produced in an anonymous white and maroon colour scheme, it was joined in 1973 by a yellow version in the yellow PTT livery of Swiss postbuses — hardly appropriate, but an attractive model for the Swiss market.

Dinky Toys' virtual monopoly of the 4mm scale diecast market was occasionally threatened by often crude models from other makers, but the first serious competition came from Corgi Toys, whose first bus (in 1961) was based on the 85mph BMMO-built CM5 coaches built for Midland Red's early services using the newly-built M1 motorway between Birmingham and London. Corgi had chosen a model that was certainly in the public eye, but which was hardly representative of current British coach design, at that time moving to 36ft-long vehicles like the Bedford VAL, and the AEC Reliance and Leyland Leopard.

Corgi also chose to include the London Transport Routemaster in its range, and this was regarded as a better (if larger) model than the equivalent Dinky. The Routemaster still

figures in the Corgi range, in a variety of liveries — but more of that anon.

Dinky stuck with its rather more representative range — Atlantean, Routemaster, Bedford VAL — through much of the 1960s, but by the early 1970s these were needing to be replaced. The first new model was not really a replacement; if you discount the Wayne School Bus (and most people did) there had never been a real single-deck bus in the range.

In 1971 this was corrected with another London model, representing an AEC Merlin with MCW body in Red Arrow livery. Here was the type of bus that London Transport's controversial reshaping report forecast would dominate London's streets for years to come. As we know, the Merlins and Swifts were not LT's most successful buses, and London quickly — perhaps *too* quickly — reverted to double-deckers, but the Red Arrow was an attractive model and appeared both in London red and a metallic red.

Next came a model of a Duple Viceroy 37 coach, very typical of the period. This was introduced by Dinky in 1972, and in 1973 a Swiss PTT version was added. At ¹⁄₉₅th scale it was much smaller than other Dinky buses, and the standard wheels appeared overscale.

The Dinky Atlantean model had disappeared from the market after 1968, and in 1973 a new Atlantean was produced, based on designs produced for the SELNEC authority in the Manchester area. It was a squarer, more clean-cut model, and survived to the end of Dinky Toys in 1979. It first appeared in an all-over advertising livery, still a comparative

novelty at the time, for Yellow Pages, to be joined in 1974 by Kenning versions in various colours and in 1977 by a Silver Jubilee version.

By this time Dinky Toys was in trouble. The company's reliance on diecast models in a fast-changing world forced the closure of the famous Binns Road factory in Liverpool in 1979, and with the factory went the name — at least until 1988, when a new range of Dinky Toys appeared. Just at the end, Dinky was planning to introduce a new model, a Continental Tourer Coach; this turned out to be neither continental nor coach, but an American Grumman Flexible 870 city bus. It was perhaps just as well that the model did not appear, as the real 870 was a singularly unsuccessful bus. In the final Dinky Toys catalogue, issued in 1979, the model was shown in a 'livery' for Liverpool Football Club, of all things, with a note that it would be 'available in alternative Football Club liveries'.

Other manufacturers were ready and willing to step into the Dinky breach, notably Corgi and Matchbox. The Matchbox commitment to buses in 4mm scale has been less than enthusiastic, basically consisting of a rather crude and under-detailed model purporting to be a London DMS-type Daimler Fleetline. This has even been produced in left-hand drive form in West Berlin livery, no doubt to confuse German children.

Matchbox did restore the balance with a bus in its Models of Yesteryear range. In 1983 it introduced a fair model of a LGOC S-type of 1922 vintage, and this has appeared in various acceptable liveries, not to mention a Kellogg's Rice Krispies promotion; the fact that everyone from cereal manufacturers to mail order catalogues is choosing to offer limited edition diecast models is a clear indication of how the perceived value of these models is growing.

Corgi's attitude to the model bus market has been markedly different, quickly appreciating the apparently unlimited appetite among collectors for different versions of the vehicles represented in its range. While in their heyday Dinky Toys were bought to be played with, it is reasonable to guess than many Corgis are kept in their boxes in pristine condition by their owners — more typically adults rather than 10-year-old boys. And few Corgis are being defaced with plasticine and Woolworth's paint.

The staple Corgi products have been the Routemaster and a Plaxton Paramount coach. The ever-safe Routemaster has appeared in a bewildering range of liveries, both in closed top and open-top guises. A few of the liveries have actually been appropriate — London Transport Omnibus 150, Shoplinker — and others have been *almost* appropriate, like British European Airways and London Country. In terms of accuracy, the kindest thing that can be said about the rest of the Routemaster variations is that they are fun.

Strangly, Corgi seems happy to produce Routemasters in a fascinating array of unrepresentative liveries, yet seems unprepared to develop models in the colours of the growing band of operators who now operate the model. I know of at least one real Routemaster operator who found Corgi unwilling to produce a commercially-available model in his company's colours — a model that would undoubtedly sell,

to judge from the interest shown in second-hand RMs.

I experienced the same attitude with the Plaxton Paramount coach. Here was an attractive model of a coach that was familiar on Britain's roads, firstly produced in National Express and Rapide liveries, quite reasonably, and then in a variety of less appropriate colours. In my professional capacity I approached Corgi to produce a Scottish Citylink version, representing vehicles that had become familiar throughout Britain. After negotiations involving supply of colour photographs and paint samples, Corgi decided at the 11th hour not to proceed. Maybe Corgi felt that Citylink was less of a national name than the liveries that have been issued — like Global and Club Cantabrica. As you might have guessed, the Routemaster operator was also Scottish-based.

To be fair, Corgi's commitment to the model bus market is generally most welcome. The range of larger-scale Corgi Classics released in the 1980s has certainly kept the collectors happy. The Thornycroft double-deck bus, sharing a chassis with other Corgi models, but with a very attractive and appropriate body, has appeared in more than half a dozen liveries relevant to fleets that operated early double-deckers, if not necessarily Thornycrofts.

The early photographs of the prototype Corgi Bedford OB model showed an ill-proportioned coach in an anachronistic yellow Bluebird livery. The models themselves proved to be very much better. The first batch of models in 1987 carried Alexanders, Grey Cars, Norfolks and Royal Blue liveries, and if they were not absolutely accurate they were, as Stan Freberg once succinctly put it, 'close enough for jazz'. Further releases in 1988 included Crosville, Eastern Counties, Premier Travel, South Midland and Southdown, and the OB model will doubtless run and run, rather like the real thing.

A rather more dubious model was Corgi's AEC Bus, which proved to be nothing more than a Routemaster with an AEC exposed radiator. It is difficult to get excited about this model, but at least the operators chosen for the range were AEC operators, which operated vehicles *vaguely* like this. The most convincing are possibly the Newcastle and Nottingham buses, not dissimilar to the real thing; least convincing is the Glasgow bus, in colours that few Glaswegians would recognise, even on a Saturday night.

Corgi's most recent models have filled a couple of gaps in the selection available. The Ford Transit minibus is not unattractive, even though the liveries (Badgerline, Bluebird and South Wales) are not strictly appropriate. A *real* minibus, maybe a Renault S56 or a Metrorider, would doubtless be more welcome, but the high cost of an entirely new model — around £40,000 — may have prompted Corgi to adapt an existing van model.

The MCW Metrobus fills the gap that existed for a good modern rear-engined double-decker. There is the Matchbox Londoner and the rather unconvincing and disappointing smaller-scale Leyland Olympian in Lledo's Marathon range, but the Metrobus is a worthy successor to the traditions of the Dinky 29c. Initially in West Midland Timesaver, West Midlands Travel and Reading Goldline liveries — all appropriate — it is doubtless set to appear in a range of colours, although the number of 'pure' Metrobus owners is quite small.

Diecast tramcar models have been rare, but Corgi took the plunge in 1088 with its Tramlines range. In the same way that tramcar builders at the turn of the century had proprietary designs that were adapted for the needs of different customers, Corgi has taken a basic tramcar lower deck which can then be adapted into various permutations. The initial models were single-deckers in Sheffield and Southampton colours, open-top double-deckers in Blackpool and London County Council colours, and closed-top double-deckers in Glasgow and Leeds colours. As these were mainly big fleets, big enough to buy or build tramcars to their own designs, none of the models looks entirely convincing, but as reproductions of typical early electric tramcars they are fine. They can also be motorised to run on OO gauge electric track, and I have no doubt that modellers have already been busy 'improving' them to suit their layouts.

The diecast business has changed dramatically over the past 30 or 40 years. From Dinkys, toys that were made to be played with — and ruined with plasticine and red paint — we now have Corgi with models to be collected in a range of colours and variations that must tax the wallet of even the most dedicated collector. In smaller scale we have Lledo's Models of Days Gone, with an anonymous normal control bus, a halfcab AEC single-decker, a Tilling ST-type AEC Regent and a Greyhound Scenicruiser coach, all models that have appeared in liveries from the sublime to the ridiculous. And this situation is aggravated by the popularity of promotional models, short-run diecasts liveried for everyone from local newspapers to building societies.

Above:
Comparing the famous and much-loved Dinky 29c double-decker — here with AEC radiator — with the newly-introduced Dinky Routemaster in 1964. Like many model buses, the excellent Routemaster casting was let down by clumsy detail, particularly at the front end. *Dinky Toys*

Many collectors are resisting the temptation to collect every bus model going, perhaps on the advice of their bank managers, and some are turning to the cheaper models which can provide a useful basis for adaptation. London souvenir shops seem to be bursting with Routemaster models of variable quality, but one which is worth finding is the Seerol version.

Variations in scale also provide problems. With early Dinky buses in roundly $\frac{1}{76}$th scale, the appearance of the larger-scale Supertoys coaches in the 1960s was regarded as a nuisance, and even today we have the inconsistencies of Corgi's Metrobus in $\frac{1}{72}$nd scale, the contemporary Transit minibus in $\frac{1}{43}$rd scale, and the Bedford OB in $\frac{1}{50}$th scale. But I suppose we should not complain. After all, there is a wide range of models on the market, mostly accurate, and since fewer people actually *play* with model buses these days, inconsistent scales are less important.

It is probably true that our needs as bus enthusiasts differ from those of model collectors. We look for replicas of buses and coaches we know, while collectors may revel in the sheer variety, accurate or not. When so much investment goes into developing a new diecast model, it seems a pity to introduce it in unsuitable or anachronistic liveries — or worse, to ignore appropriate liveries in favour of some of the strange confections that have appeared.

The lead time for *Buses Year Book* means that this is written some months before you read it — but at the time of writing there are still no Corgi Routemasters in the liveries of real fleets like Clydeside, Kelvin, Magicbus, Strathtay, Cumberland, Blackpool, United Counties or Southampton — and the fact that a Corgi East Yorkshire Routemaster has been on the market for some time is quite unconnected with East Yorkshire's move to RMs in 1988.

With the undoubted benefit of hindsight, you can see the buses that have been missed, the models that would have been more representative than those chosen by the manufacturers.

Where, in the 1950s, was a Bristol Lodekka model? Here was a standard bus that could be seen from Inverness to Cornwall, but which never found its way into a diecast range. Maybe a Corgi Classic of the future?

Or its stablemate the Bristol RELL, a much-loved and familiar vehicle. Or, even more significantly the Leyland National, which peaked when Dinky was in trouble, but which would have been a more acceptable model throughout the country than the Red Arrow. Perhaps the manufacturers of today will recognise the Leyland Lynx as a potentially attractive model, even though its sales are not in the National class. After all, it has already outsold the Duple Roadmaster and Harrington Contender.

Simon Butler

New Look in Northumbria

Northumbria Motor Services was created in 1986 from the northern part of United Automobile Services. It immediately created a dramatic new identity using a red, grey and white livery applied in an unorthodox style. **Simon Butler** *illustrates a selection of Northumbria's vehicles.*

Below:
There are nine MCW Metroliner double-deckers in the Northumbria fleet. All were originally in National Express white, but this example seen at Victoria, London, is in fleet livery. Since this photograph was taken in August 1987 this bus has been reregistered with an appropriate Northumberland Motor Services number, **NMS 700.**

Facing page, top:
The oddest vehicle to receive Northumbria livery —
albeit in a simplified style — is this driver training
bus. New to East Kent in 1966 it is a Park
Royal-bodied AEC Regent V.

Facing page, bottom:
As an alternative to buying new coaches in 1987 the
company sent five 10-year-old Leyland Leopards to
Hestair Duple to be rebodied. They were fitted with
55-seat 320 bodies suitable for local bus operation
with two-piece doors and the provision to carry
ticket-issuing equipment. Their original S-suffix
registrations were replaced by numbers in the SV
series to disguise the age of the chassis.

Left:
Double-deck additions in 1987 were eight ex-Greater
Manchester Daimler Fleetlines, the first of the type in
the fleet, although they did have the same Gardner
6LXB power unit as used in the company's Olympians
and later Bristol VRTs. All had Northern Counties
bodywork.

Below:
The newest buses in the fleet when it was formed
were a pair of C-registered Leyland Olympians with
ECW bodywork with 72 coach seats. They were part of
a batch of six buses, the other four of which remained
with United. New Olympians, but with Alexander
bodywork, were purchased in 1988. Behind is the
oldest bus in the fleet in 1988, a 1972 Leyland National
originally operated by Northern General.

Left:
There are nine ex-Midland Red North Nationals in the fleet, acquired in 1987. This one is seen loading in Blyth, with an ex-United National 2 in the background.

Below:
Bristol VRTs and LHs were standard fare in the United fleet and a number of each passed to Northumbria. The two VRTs nearest the camera are standard United-specification buses with ECW bodies and Gardner 6LX engines. On the extreme left is a 1979 LH with 43-seat ECW body, while alongside is a 1977 example, one of a pair which started life with Western National and joined the United fleet in 1984.

Right:
Northumbria's first new buses were 60 Freight Rover Sherpa 16-seaters delivered in 1987. Most had Dormobile bodies, including this one loading at St Mary's lighthouse in August 1988.

Below:
The Sherpas were followed by 45 MCW Metroriders with 25-seat dual-purpose bodies. This one is seen at Four Lane Ends, Newcastle, but during 1988 examples were to be found operating as far afield as Glasgow, on loan to Strathclyde Buses, and Kent, running for Northumbria's sister company, Kentish Bus.

Merseyside Liveries

Merseyside, more than any other Passenger Transport Executive, had frequent changes of mind on its bus livery, trying both different shades and different layouts of green and cream. It was only in 1988 that the PTE's successor company, Merseybus, finally broke away from the green which had been part of Liverpool's bus scene since the war. Local photographer **Reg Wilson** *shows some examples of how the liveries have changed.*

Right:
Typical of Merseyside PTE in the early 1970s is this all-over green livery, relieved only by cream surrounds to the side windows — a livery inherited from Liverpool City Transport. This is a 1973 East Lancs-bodied Leyland Atlantean, photographed when new. An Alexander-bodied Atlantean follows.

Below right:
When the PTE was formed the buses acquired from the two Wirral municipal fleets — Birkenhead and Wallasey — received a blue and cream livery, to allay local concern about a Liverpool takeover. The blue represented Birkenhead, the cream, Wallasey, and it was applied in the style shown here on a 1951 Leyland Titan PD2 with old-fashioned looking Metro-Cammell bodywork. This was in fact the first bus to receive the Wirral livery and it is seen here in March 1970 soon after being repainted. It was withdrawn in 1972.

Above:

In 1974 the PTE absorbed the bus fleets of St Helens and Southport and for a time retained red and cream liveries for both towns. Some buses were even transferred from other divisions and repainted red, including this ex-Birkenhead Massey-bodied PD2/40 seen in St Helens in May 1974. The Merseyside name in the box was shortlived; the previous logo was soon reintroduced, accompanied by the fleetname Merseyside Transport.

Left:

The Wirral livery layout with a broad area of cream set the standard for the rest of the fleet — but using light green and cream. An ex-Birkenhead Atlantean in green and cream at Woodside Ferry in 1976 also shows the Merseyside Transport fleetname used from the mid-1970s. It has 71-seat Northern Counties bodywork.

Left:
Inter-division transfers saw this former Birkenhead Leyland Leopard at work in Southport in 1976 in Verona green and cream. The two-door 42-seat body was by Massey. New in 1964, this bus was withdrawn from service in 1977. The tower behind marks the entrance to Ribble's Lord Street bus station, now closed.

Above:
The PTE had a commendable sense of history and was not averse to repainting buses in traditional liveries. On the left in this 1979 photograph is an Atlantean with Metro-Cammell body in 1929 Wallasey livery. The Alexander-bodied Atlantean on the right is in Birkenhead livery from the same year.

Right:
From 1978 the PTE's livery settled down to green and cream with brown relief. This Derby Transport Ailsa was operated on loan for six months in 1982 and had 79-seat bodywork by Marshall. The PTE retained a divisional structure and this was marked by different coloured logos — dark blue in the case of this Wirral bus.

Left:

The formation of Merseyside Transport in 1986 saw the introduction of the Merseybus fleetname on the existing green, cream and brown livery. An Ailsa with Alexander R-type body illustrates this in West Kirby in 1988.

Below left:

Merseyside Travel adopted the fleetname Merseycoach for its coach fleet, made up mainly of Leyland Tigers. This is a 1982 model with Duple Dominant IV bodywork at Southport. The livery is two-tone green and cream.

Bottom left:

The company's small fleet of minibuses received the Merseymini name. This is an Alexander-bodied Dodge S56. Similar buses were received from Northern Counties.

Above right:

At the end of 1987 the search began for a new livery and 20 buses were painted two-tone green, including this 1976 Leyland Atlantean with East Lancs 75-seat bodywork. The overall effect was rather drab.

Right:

In April 1988 there came a completely new livery — maroon and cream. The first buses to be delivered in it were 15 Leyland Olympians with Northern Counties bodies. Alexander-bodied Olympians followed later in the year. The upswept paint line behind the rearmost side windows copies the appearance of the valances above the engine compartment on Alexander-bodied Atlanteans — ironic in view of the preoccupation 25 years earlier with trying to disguise the engine compartment by building the valances out to give Atlanteans and Fleetlines an unbroken rear profile. The deep cream front panel is designed to make the buses distinctive at night.

Bus Stations

The good, the bad, and the ugly.
Peter Rowlands *discusses bus stations
from the viewpoint of the camera-carrying
enthusiast.*

Let's face it, taking photographs in bus stations is an admission of defeat. I mean, it's such an *obvious* thing to do, isn't it? 'You'll never believe what I saw in the bus station. Yes — a bus.' Bound to slay them, that is.

Yet we all take pictures in bus stations, don't we? It's like a curse that's been wished on us — a

forfeit we all have to pay to join the game. Ten per cent of your pictures will be taken in bus stations. By decree.

But haven't you cursed the inconvenience of it? Burrowing down to the murky depths of Newcastle-upon-Tyne's Eldon Centre bus station, and peering through the diesel-laden

murk for some sign of usable light? Or weaving frantically through the subterranean warren of Northampton's Greyfriars concourse, trying to reach the other end before that Olympian up on the surface?

Think how much time you've wasted sitting on a wall at one end of Swansea bus station (or somewhere like it), waiting to photograph a bus that left 20 minutes ago through the other exit. Or wrestling with the railings Burnley uses to pen in would-be passengers, trying to get a clear view between the bars.

And what about all those passengers? Unsympathetic bystanders who wouldn't dream of moving three-seventeenths of an inch to their left, even if you've been standing mute and motionless for 5 minutes with your camera poised. You need them, of course, to add colour to the occasion; but not to the extent that they completely obliterate the view.

Then when you finally have the photograph developed, what do you find? A boring picture of an empty bus standing all by itself against a brick wall.

Why do we put up with it? It's bad enough for the travellers actually using the bus services; for them, the bus station may be the only option. But we with our cameras can go where we like. What draws us here?

To be fair, some people actually enjoy bus stations. Like railway stations, they are a gateway to other worlds. They carry a hint of the same sense of adventure and uncertainty. And to the diehard enthusiast, they are mini-Meccas in themselves — places that are guaranteed to have buses in them, in all their sheet metal and mechanical awesomeness. They form an ideal backdrop for an obsession.

But the parallel with railway stations isn't too convincing — especially not if it's local bus stations you're talking about. I mean, domestic-sounding destinations such as Woodside or Hillside or Witton aren't going to set the blood tingling like Penzance or Inverness, are they? Hardly the stuff of epic journeys or heroic deeds.

Besides, bus stations differ from railway stations in a more fundamental way. They're optional where train stations are obligatory; you don't have to go to one to board a bus. Admittedly, you may have little choice if the bus station is the focal point of all the local services; but even then, you can usually be pretty certain that the bus will be stopping again somewhere down the street. You don't get trains doing that.

Above:
Saw-tooth platforms usually make photography difficult with guard rails, queues and other buses conspiring to get in the way. An unobstructed view like this is rare, but the clutter cannot be entirely eliminated.

Right:
Back-lighting, a low viewpoint and a distant Routemaster add interest to Newark's island platform bus station.

Left:
On the approach to temporary bus stands in central Wigan, a GM Buses Volvo Citybus with Northern Counties body negotiates road reconstruction.

The illogical thing is, bus stations vary in importance from one town to the next. Go to Chatham, for instance, and you're drawn to that towering monolith at the bottom of the hill. It's dark inside the elevated bus station, of course, but you can always pick out buses on the ramp; and that's where they all seem to go. Yet along the road at neighbouring Maidstone, the bus station is a relative backwater — somewhere to check out when you've had your fill of buses on the street.

Often, it's this contrast that decides whether or not you gravitate to the bus station. If you spill out from your car or coach or train into streets bereft of buses, then the bus station is the obvious answer. If there are buses everywhere you look, it's less of a priority.

Sometimes the bus station is especially optional. Manchester's Piccadilly bus station, for instance, throngs with buses all day long, but there are plenty of them on the surrounding streets, too. Your visit wouldn't be a disaster if you ignored it completely. Sheffield's central bus station is much the same; in fact I may as well confess that for years I never even knew it

was there. The same applies to Newcastle-upon-Tyne's Haymarket bus station — still open-air, unlike the Eldon; it's a good gathering point, but it's not essential viewing.

Yet cross the river to Gateshead and you find a different situation. The bus station at the Metro interchange is like a magnet, drawing in all the buses that pass. It would be a waste to visit the town without calling there. Apart from anything else, it has a commanding view across the Tyne, and it's overlooked by a grassy slope from which you can often get some useful shots of parked vehicles.

That Gateshead location is reasonably photogenic; and this in itself can sometimes be a reason for taking pictures in bus stations. Consider for instance the one in Newcastle-under-Lyme. I was fascinated when I first called there 10 years ago by a concrete building overlooking it, with a façade of strange, interwoven arches. It could brighten up a picture of even the most mundane vehicle.

Or look at the bus station at Cwmbran in South Wales. For many years it was relatively drab and featureless, set as it was against the

austere concrete of the new town centre. Now, thanks to someone's efforts to improve its image, one end of it sports a vast, outrageous glass canopy supported by a latticework of broad blue steel tubes. It was calculated to be stunning, and it is.

Even if the bus station itself isn't particularly interesting, it's always legitimate to take photographs in it when they're your Only Hope. For instance, this was the case when I found myself in Bury one day two summers ago, in between appointments. Bury is one of those towns where the bus station is a bit of a focal point, so I was hanging around it, looking out for anything interesting. And sure enough, what should pull in but a single-deck Leyland Fleetline that had been rebuilt from a double-decker after an accident.

Now the ideal approach would have been to wait for it to leave and then photograph it in the street outside. But I simply couldn't take chances with such a rare vehicle. After all, which way would it turn when it left? Would the sun be in the right place? Anyway, when was it going? I had only 10 minutes to spare. Well, the

driver told me it was leaving in 20 minutes, so I might have pushed my luck and waited. But weighing everything up, I decided to bang off a few shots where it stood, and be on my way. The sun was right for both front and rear views, and all in all I counted myself quite lucky.

The same thing happened to me in Newark not long ago, in pursuit of Gash's Routemasters. I photographed those all right in Newark's narrow streets, but inevitably I wended my way to the bus station. And sure enough, an ex-Manchester Leyland Titan promptly rolled in and stopped by the bus shelter, facing the sun. Well, the light would be wrong for vehicles pulling out; and besides, the Titan looked great where it was. Go on — tell me I was wrong.

There's no denying, though, that lack of movement can be a bit of a problem in bus stations. After all, most of the time the buses in them are standing still. If you're poised among the would-be passengers, I suppose the classic remedy is to wait until the bus has just drawn back from the rank, ready to swing off. The brakes groan, escaping air hisses, the shutter

clicks. That is, providing another bus hasn't charged up and obscured the view.

But some bus stations are big enough to offer some fairly dramatic movement within their confines — especially if you've got a long lens to pull the action in close. Glasgow's Buchanan bus station is a prime example — although taking pictures through that famous exit on Parliamentary Road has become a bit of a cliché in itself.

Still, you could argue that pictures of buses leaving bus stations are as legitimate as those taken out on the street. Certainly you can get plenty of movement then. As for pictures of buses arriving — well, if you angle the camera right, only an expert could tell the bus station was there. (On the other hand, you've got to face the fact that it's probably only experts who will have any interest anyway.)

In the past, one good reason for avoiding bus stations was the fact that they were generally so depressing. If some evil genius had wanted to roll together all that was most ugly in postwar British architecture, he couldn't have done it more effectively than by presenting us with

some of our worst bus stations. Maybe one day the precast concrete shelters, the drab iron-mongery, the stained cement will be looked on with reverence by social historians; at the moment they're an insult to the people who have to endure them.

Happily, things have brightened considerably where local authorities have made some invest-ment. Have a look at Leicester St Margarets, for instance, with its bright modern façade, its paved circulating area and its clean, airy covered concourse. Or look at Merthyr Tydfil, where they've facelifted the existing building and replaced the old shelters with trim, arched ones in unbreakable glass. The place no longer smacks of Merthyr, Industrial Relic. It suggests something more like Merthyr, Gateway to Mid-Wales.

Not that the planners always get it right. One of the most impressive modern bus stations is at Bradford Interchange: smart concourses, shel-tered waiting, escalators galore. The only problem is, not enough people want to inter-change there.

Or look at the bus station at Milton Keynes — a ridiculously overblown modern edifice with practically nothing worth talking about inside. Moreover, to reach it from the adjacent railway station you're faced with an exposed and inconvenient walk across an open square and a road. As for the town centre, that's a minibus ride away. But where do you pick up the minibuses to get there? Not at the railway station entrance. Not at the bus station either (too far away). No, you board them at ordinary bus stops out on the main road. (Incidently, as I

write this the Milton Keynes buses are a bit of a disappoinment in themselves. Whoever dreamed up a white, yellow and grey livery? It makes them look as though they're doing their utmost to avoid being seen.)

Even updating has not yet cured all the problems of traditional bus stations. Too many of them still suffer from pervasive litter and general dowdiness. And even where improve-ments have been made, too often the impression that lingers is of smoke-laden cafes with stained Formica table-tops and slippery floors. Maybe a nation gets the bus stations it deserves.

But if so, maybe we should be trying harder. After all, a properly managed and well sited bus station can lift the whole image of bus travel. It may not be ideal for an enthusiast, but you've got to be fair. From the passenger's point of view there's a world of difference between queuing in the street for a bus that might never arrive, and waiting in comfort in a bright, covered concourse with announcements and information displays and a general air of purposefulness. That kind of bus station can make you feel welcome, and give you some reassurance that your bus might actually come.

The worrying thing is that since deregulation and the National Bus sell-off, the potential profits of redevelopment have put many bus stations under threat. The tide of opinion seems to have swung against them, and in some cases self-help seems to mean going back to waiting in the street. Even when bus stations are offered as part of some grandiose development plan, too often they seem like an afterthought, plunged in the depths of an office or shopping complex

Bus stations are useful for tracking down oddities. GM Buses' unique single-deck Fleetline pauses on a loading bay in Bury's bus-rail interchange.

Above:
Chester's bus station features an attractive paved surface complemented by shelters with arched roofs. A Chester Dominator, acquired from Merthyr Tydfil Transport loads in front of a Renault minibus. The Dominator has Marshall Camair bodywork; the Renault has a Northern Counties body.

Left:
Yorkshire Rider's lowheight Fleetlines have long been a part of the scene at Burnley's surprisingly large bus station. This one, 16 years old when photographed, sets off for Halifax.

Left:
Weardale's Plaxton-bodied Leopard bus, waiting to leave Bishop Auckland's modern bus station, shows no sign of its age when photographed in 1988. It was new in 1965.

Below left:
Stourbridge bus station is one of the few to be overlooked by a ruined castle. A West Midlands Travel MCW Metrobus II leaves for Birmingham.

Below:
The author's local bus station allowed interesting comparisons such as this until 1988 when Routemasters disappeared from Enfield. RM5 arrives from Central London while a Metrobus waits to leave for Waltham Cross.

where neither travellers nor photographers can find much joy.

Perhaps the smaller local bus stations are the most satisfactory in some ways — lacking the worst pretensions and blemishes of their larger counterparts, yet often providing a rallying point for any number of photographic endeavours. At Little Park Gardens, my local bus station in Enfield (nothing more really than a nicely-paved yard), I have photographed Routemasters arriving and leaving from almost every possible angle. They've gone from there now, though they survived until late 1988, so I'm not sorry for my efforts; only that an era has drifted inexorably past.

And you never know — one day I may actually go there to catch a bus.

Roy Marshall

Full Front Double-Deckers

In an effort to improve the lopsided appearance of traditional halfcab double-deckers small numbers of operators have over the years opted for full-width cabs, generally giving a cleaner appearance and some hint of modernity. Their main drawback was the added structure impeding access to the engine. **Roy Marshall** illustrates some of the operators which opted for full fronts on double-deckers.

Sunderland Corporation was buying streamlined trams in the 1930s and was clearly anxious to improve the looks of its buses. Two Crossley Mancunians delivered in 1937 were given full-fronted bodies by English Electric. The streamlined paint scheme was eye-catching, but the heavy old-fashioned Crossley radiator effectively defeated any attempts to make these centre entrance buses look modern.

Midland Red, designing and building its own buses in the 1930s, specified a full-front for one of its FEDD models in 1938. The end result was perhaps better than in Sunderland despite the rather square outline of the body, although the symmetry of the cab highlights the offset location of the radiator. Brush built the body on this, the only FEDD to have a full front. The poor engine access was no doubt an important factor for Midland Red's practical engineers.

Blackpool Corporation was specifying full fronts on its new buses in the late 1930s and doubtless influenced neighbouring Lytham St Annes to follow suit. Four TD5s were delivered in 1937 with standard highbridge Leyland bodies but with full fronts which looked particularly neat, helped no doubt by the Leyland radiator which was almost flush with the body panels.

Above:
Blackpool's prewar Titans had full fronts and exposed radiators. The postwar versions had bodywork which differed little in design from the earlier vehicles but which benefitted from having a concealed radiator. There were 100 of these attractive PD2s with centre entrance Burlingham bodies which fitted well with Blackpool's holiday image.

Left:
Full fronts are often associated with seaside towns and Bournemouth was another coastal municipality to specify them both before and after World War 2. Bournemouth's decision was no doubt influenced by its operation of trolleybuses which, with their smooth fronts, usually looked more modern than motorbuses. In 1950 a fleet of 30 PD2/3s with Weymann dual-door and dual-staircase bodies was purchased by Bournemouth. The shallow cab windows and the high lower edge of the front panel made them look a trifle ungainly.

Above:

This Highland Omnibus Guy Arab III was a Motor Show exhibit and for many years was the newest double-decker in the company's fleet. It had a Strachans body and was one of the few full-fronted double-deckers to be purchased new by a Scottish operator. The exuberant streamlining on Highland's rather drab red livery owed more to the 1930s than to the 1950s. It entered service in 1952.

Right:

Ribble by contrast had some particularly stylish full-front PD2s. These were the White Ladies, double-deck coaches used on express services in Lancashire. There were two batches, one bodied by East Lancs of Blackburn and one by Burlingham of Blackpool. This is an East Lancs-bodied vehicle, new in 1951. Note the deep windscreens and the stylish front complete with bumpers flanking the registration plate.

Left:
Industrial Walsall seems an unlikely setting for full-fronted buses but the Corporation bought such bodywork from both Park Royal and Roe. The Roe-bodied buses were 10 PD2/12s which entered service in 1953. Note the platform doors and the sliding cab door on the nearside.

Below:
Edinburgh's only full-fronted buses were not quite what they seemed — the nearside was unglazed and there was a conventional bonnet behind the built-up front panel. This was a wartime Daimler, rebodied in 1954 by Alexander and one of that coachbuilder's first orders from Scotland's capital.

Above:
Southdown went in for full fronts in a big way in the late 1950s and early 1960s on Leyland Titan PD3 chassis. But before standardising on PD3s it had one PD2 delivered with a fully-fronted Northern Counties body. The deep cab side windows were attractive, but the front end with its sun visor and plain grille were less so.

Left:
The standard Southdown fully-fronted double-decker perhaps suffered from its shallow windscreens and plain grille. Interesting features of the body were the short central bay and the rearmost side window, curved to match that on the top deck. Southdown bought 285 PD3s like this, and generally similar bodies were supplied by Northern Counties to a number of other operators including Barton Transport, AA Motor Services, A1 Service, Garelochhead Coach Services and Middlesbrough Corporation.

Left:
Ribble, which like Southdown was part of the British Electric Traction group, also went for fully-fronted PD3s but with bodywork by Burlingham (as seen here) and later by Metro-Cammell. A total of 236 were purchased. Note that Ribble opted for a sliding door rather than the double-jacknife type used by Southdown. One Burlingham body of this type was supplied on a Guy Arab to Wolverhampton Corporation.

Above:
Wolverhampton bought 50 Arabs in 1960-61 with Metro-Cammell full front bodies. Later Arabs reverted to conventional halfcabs and, unusually, one of the full-fronted examples was rebuilt with a halfcab.

UK buyers of new full-fronted double-deck bus bodies

† prewar   * postwar

*   AA Motor Services, Ayr
*   A1 Services, Ardrossan
*   Barton Transport
† * Blackpool Corporation
*   Bolton Corporation
† * Bournemouth Corporation
*   East Kent Road Car Co
*   Edinburgh Corporation
*   Garelochhead Coach Services
*   Highland Transport
*   Liverpool Corporation
†   Lytham St Annes Corporation
*   Middlesbrough Corporation
†   Midland Red
*   Ribble Motor Services
†   Sheffield Transport
*   Silcox, Pembroke Dock
*   Southdown Motor Services
†   Sunderland Corporation
*   Ulster Transport Authority
*   Walsall Corporation
†   West Hartlepool Corporation
*   Wolverhampton Corporation

Left and below left:
Perhaps the most bizarre full front double-deckers were run by Silcox of Pembroke Dock. Both were Bristol Ks and one had a body built by Silcox which might actually have looked better with a conventional halfcab. The Silcox-bodied bus had a concealed radiator while the other (below left), fitted with a prewar Metro-Cammell body removed from a Birmingham Corporation trolleybus, had an exposed radiator and turned out to be a reasonably attractive ensemble.

Below:
The ultimate development of the full-fronted double-deck body was the stylish design built by Northern Counties for Barton Transport which had curved windscreens, giving the buses a modern appearance unmatched by the contemporary box-like bodies on rear-engined chassis. Most were on AEC Regent V chassis, but this one was a lowbridge body mounted on a low-height Dennis Loline III, giving an overall height of around 12ft 6in. It was bought for a route between Nottingham and Castle Donnington but spent most of its life on the nonstop route X42 from Nottingham to Derby.